LETTERS FROM THE ATTIC

GREGG CONDON

MARSH LAKE PRODUCTIONS

ISBN: 0-9637697-1-5

LETTERS FROM THE ATTIC

DEDICATION

This book is dedicated to my wife, Kathy. She shared with me the arduous summertime task of cleaning out the old un-airconditioned home. Day after day she and I enjoyed the discovery of the bundles of old letters as we worked in the attic.

Kathy was my partner in the first reading of the letters. I read them aloud, every one, while Kathy listened for content and made organizational notes. The letters were handled with reverence and care, and we read them mostly on winter evenings while sitting by our fireplace. These times together will always be remembered for their special qualities.

Gregg Condon

PROLOGUE

There is a greatness of spirit inherent in the human heart which transcends status, wealth, or power. Everyone--from those of the loftiest station to the most humbly endowed--may possess it. It is a commodity free to all who can comprehend it, and its storehouse is the human soul.

LETTERS FROM THE ATTIC is the chronicle of six generations of one family and their role in the "Great Experiment" of the American republic. More to the point, it is a testament to the human spirit and the triumph of the "better angels" of human nature.

LETTERS FROM THE ATTIC is a compilation of the family writings found in this home. Here Hannah and Addie Smith are pictured in front of their home in the 1890s.

PART ONE

THE CONTEXT OF THE LETTERS

Part One is the context of the letters. The letters from the old attic tell the story of the American experience. Their details define the times in which the writers lived. Their spirit defines the writers themselves. It is a deep and stirring insight into who Americans have been since the first of the letters was written in 1853.

In establishing the context of the letters, attention is given to the home in which the letters were discovered, the discovery of the letters themselves, and the family who wrote the letters.

CHAPTER ONE

THE HOME

Smith's new home was lovely--as lovely as a home can be. From its outward appearance, to its innermost rooms and corridors, it possessed an undeniable *something*. "Warmth," was the word visitors most often chose when trying to describe the emotional impact which the home had on them. Had the home been a person, rather than an object of masonry and wood, it would have been acclaimed to have a personality that could be described only as *charismatic*.

Lest the image abuilding in the reader's mind grow too grand, it must be said that the house was by no means a mansion. It was grand and lovely, not in its pretensions, but rather in the honest elegance of what it was.

Built in 1877 by Francis and Hannah Smith, the home's architecture followed the Italianate lines. Low sloping roofs featured wide eves which were supported by intricate scrollwork brackets. Multiple roof lines stepped down one from another in a beautifully cascading symmetry, each portion of the home having its unique height--north wing, south wing, kitchen, woodshed room, bay window, and two porches.

The foundation was of native yellow-gray limestone, with the walls of "Cream City" Milwaukee yellow brick. Windows were tall and arch-topped. Woodwork and trim were painted white from the day the house was new, while shutters were green and the tin roof was silver. And, being keepers of traditions, successive generations of the family saw to it that these things never changed.

Behind the house stood a matching brick two-story horse and carriage barn, which would have done justice to a mansion, had it been the companion of one. And, near the barn a brick outhouse originally reposed--architecturally consistent with the house, of course. The barn had been relegated to the indignity of automobile storage upon the demise of the carriage, and the outhouse had succumbed to the advent of domestic conveniences in the nineteen-teens.

Situated on a double corner lot adjacent to the small city's business district, the home was conspicuous. Stately churches faced the home across both streets of the corner intersection, and passersby would do a "double-take," then slow down for yet a closer look.

Three generations of trees grew to shade the home's stately contours. On summer afternoons the interplay of leafy shadows caused countless spots of sunlight to brighten the aging walls.

On the interior, the home was possessed of an inviting charm. For the entire length of the structure, three first-floor rooms opened into one another in a grand expanse of space and light--dining room, sitting room, and parlor. In addition to kitchen, pantry, and closets, there had originally been six bedrooms. A pair of the latter were eventually merged into one; and from the start, the back-most upstairs bedroom had been designated as the storeroom, or "the attic."

Ah, the attic. Never had its plastered walls been papered or painted. Never had it seen the installation of electric lighting or central heat. In its plain, remote confines reposed the treasures of the family. Stacked trunks, boxes, picture frames, valises, furniture, and infinite minutia filled the space nearly to the ceiling.

It was, of course, the silent repository of the letters which form the topic of this book.

CHAPTER TWO

THE DISCOVERY OF THE LETTERS

Growing up with family history and tradition was a privilege which Gregg Condon enjoyed. The old family home was more than just a place. It was a tangible bond with ancestors whose lifetimes had spanned the entirety of American history. Gregg knew who he was and what his family stood for--values far more important to him than any advantage which might accrue to the modern Americans' frequent moves which are made in quest of fleeting economic advantages.

For 120 years the same family descended the same porch steps to walk the same street to shop in the same store buildings a block away. For 120 years furniture sat in the same appointed places. By the door was a table whose wood-inlay top spelled, "Betsy Jones," grandmother of Gregg's great-grandmother and sister of John Paul Jones of Revolutionary War seafaring fame.

On the mantle was a vase from the Hale family ancestors, owned by a great-grandmother of Gregg's great-grandmother whose brother was Nathan Hale, American Revolutionary War patriot executed by the British and leaving the immortal last words: "I regret that I have but one life to give for my country."

In a corner of the parlor stood a table brought by a direct ancestor from England to Plymouth Colony in the 1620s. In the china cabinet was a hand-carved wooden pepper shaker brought from England by a "recently arrived" ancestor in 1840. Photos of family members who died before the Civil War looked down from the same antique picture frames upon the same rooms--for 120 years.

For 120 years the same family had Thanksgiving dinner, served by the same silver and on the same china, in the same dining room. For 120 years in unbroken succession, the family celebrated Christmas in the same parlor beside the same hearth.

Then it was over. Within six weeks of one another, Arnold and Joyce Condon died. Son, Gregg, and his sons had homes and livelihoods elsewhere; there was no one left to maintain the tradition of the family home in Brodhead, Wisconsin. And so in the summer of 1997, Gregg and Kathy began the sad task of dismantling 120 years of family tradition and family history.

At first their surprises were few. After all, the stories of things from pantry to parlor were well known. But when at last the investigations reached the remote upstairs attic the surprises were astonishing. Here was an Edison hand-blown light bulb from the 1890s--and it still worked!

Here was Francis Smith's military enlistment paper from 1840 written with quill pen, and the brass buttons from his uniform, and two powder horns. Here was his silver conductor's badge from 1850 when he drove horse-drawn streetcars on Broadway in New York City. Here were Abigail Davidson's schoolbooks, all dated in the 1840s--and her wooden flute.

Here was a three-foot intricately crafted miniature birch-bark canoe--along with bead-work moccasins--which Indians had traded with Francis Smith for groceries in his store a block away on Main Street.

Here, too, was a stack of newspapers announcing the Kennedy assassination, the atomic bomb, Pearl Harbor, the death of Dillinger, the abdication of the Kaiser, the assassination of Lincoln, the Gettysburg Address, the death of George Washington, and an "extra" from 1770 reporting what history came to call The Boston Massacre.

There were first-edition works of Dickens and the early American authors, the prettiest set of teacups the auctioneer had ever seen, pocket watches from five generations, an 1855 Smith & Wesson revolver (this famed company's Model Number One, no less), and an 1861 Remington. A metal chest contained an avalanche of silver dollars dating from 1840 to 1870, along with a few gold pieces and Confederate bills.

10

A hand-written family pedigree revealed the succession of parentage from the present generations running straight as an arrow back to George Soule who stepped off the Mayflower at Plymouth in 1620. There were 76 hangers full of Civil War era clothing, a merchant's display case of ancient unused clay pipes, 22 antique dolls (mostly the china-headed variety), 30 pairs of high-buttoned shoes, and 36 quilts--mostly from the 1800s. Astonishingly, there was a tablecloth in excellent condition which bore a note revealing that Gregg's great, great, great, great, great grandmother had grown the flax, spun the thread, and had woven it--and *she* had been born in 1750!

But, the greatest treasure of all was the bundles of letters. Each generation of the family had seemingly saved every letter they ever received. At various points in their lives they had carefully bundled them up and had stashed them in random places in the attic--probably quite unaware that preceding generations had done the same thing.

This book is about the letters. In a sense, this book *is* the letters. It can be asserted that they are the greatest treasure the old home held because of the wealth of information they have to offer. They are a testament to the value of family. They define what relationships are at their best. They bear witness to love of country. They express self-reliance and responsibility. And, they provide eloquent examples of how civilized people can express love, commitment, and faith.

Some of the letters are written by writers who are brilliantly masterful at the art of verbal expression. Other letters are written by people whose only eloquence was in the example set by their lives, and whose only brilliance was the radiance of their souls. Some letters written by outsiders to members of the family express cynicism, or hint at behavior not wholly ethical--but those round out the colorful spectrum of the human drama.

This book is not about the few who rose to greatness. It is about the ordinary folks--the rank-and-file citizens--who defined our civilization and gave America its highest hopes and deepest qualities.

CHAPTER THREE

THE FAMILY

A substantive bundle of old letters tells the story of the common person's American adventure over the last 140 years. It is the story of one family whose successive generations called the same place "home" for five generations. And, since the first generation to occupy the home kept letters written by their parents, six generations of the family are made known.

The First Generation

The story begins with Francis and Hannah Smith. They were both from Grafton, New York; an upstate town near Troy. Francis was born there in 1822. Francis' first wife was also born in Grafton. She was Abigail Davidson, and she and Francis were married in 1850. In 1854 they moved west to Wisconsin, residing in Whitewater before moving to Brodhead in 1859. That year she died at age 34, of causes the letters never revealed. The bill of lading for the movement of their goods to Wisconsin and the letters which followed from their families back in New York provide a fascinating insight into the language, everyday challenges, and human relationships and values of that now distant time.

Brodhead had been founded only three years prior to Abigail's death, and the region was a sparsely populated frontier. Francis went back to Grafton in search of another wife. He found Hannah Allen, a family friend of both the Smiths and the Davidsons. When they were married he was 38; she was 22. In their wedding photo his expression appears to show satisfaction while hers shows uncertainty. Hannah was a pretty young lady whose ancestors had fought in the Revolution. Typical of a girl born in 1840 she had gone to school for only three weeks. Her letters reveal a splendid human character and a decided lack of "book learning" in the ways of spelling and punctuation.

Francis returned to Brodhead with his new bride. They constructed a two-story brick business building in Brodhead's small business district. In this building the Smiths operated a grocery store. A newspaper ad from the 1880's proclaimed him to be "An Ice Creamist."

Prior to the building of their new home in 1877, the Smiths lived in a variety of places in Brodhead. During these years they had four children. The first three died of the then-common childhood diseases. They died at the ages of three months, one year, and four years. The four-year-old had a wooden rocking horse which was still in the attic at the time of the discovery of the letters.

Francis Smith was known for his good nature. He always had a merry twinkle in his eye, his mouth was always curling in anticipation of his next laugh, and he had a sincere respect for his fellow humans. When his new home was under construction, he sneaked into the site one night and buried a sackful of coal. The next day he was delighted to witness the excitement as the workmen discovered Wisconsin's first coal mine!

Francis' humor was directed at the interior of his home as well. He had a series of steps built in the main closet. The stairs ended at a blank wall, and Francis called this his "burglar closet," joking that any burglar would enter the closet and become confused at the end of the stairs which would give Francis the opportunity to trap him inside. He also had the front door lock specially made. The keyhole was in the shape of his initial--an *S*. The key, with its *S*-shaped teeth, was unique.

The Second Generation

The Smith's fourth child was a girl named Addie, born in 1875. She was two years old when the Smiths moved into their new home. Her lifetime must be remembered as civilization's era of greatest change. When she was born, Grant was President. She was a year old when Custer's Seventh Cavalry and the Sioux battled on the banks of The Little Bighorn. She was in the first grade when the Earps killed the Clantons at Tombstone's OK Corral. She was in her twenties when electricity and telephones became commonplace, she was 28 when the first airplane flew, 40 when automobiles came to outnumber horses on city streets, 52 when Lindbergh flew the Atlantic, and 70 when the first atomic bomb fell and jet planes took to the skies.

When Addie was 7, her father died. Francis was 60 and had cancer--quite untreatable in those days. Hannah was 44 when she lost her husband. Women were seldom career people then. For income she rented the store to another operator, rented out rooms in her house, and took in laundry for pay. The house still had a mortgage, and she was determined to keep her home.

Two years later Will Hyde--a devastated man from Mississippi--wandered into Brodhead in search of a new life. He had lost his plantations, wife, and seven children in the Civil War. The final destruction of his life as he'd known it had come in 1865 when he invested all his remaining money in a shipload of cotton destined for England. The ship succeeded in running the Union blockade, but Lee surrendered before the ship landed and the cotton was sold for less money than Mr. Hyde had paid for it.

In Brodhead, Mr. Hyde worked mostly as a traveling salesman but also did some auctioneering and often lent a hand with the printing presses at the *Brodhead Independent*. He and Hannah were married in 1884, and he accepted his wife's religion which was Baptist. Only a decade after their marriage, Mr. Hyde died of a stroke. Hannah was 56 and never again had a man in her life. She was so distraught at her church's lack of attention at the time of her husband's death that she switched to being a Methodist. Hannah lived to be 82--the family's beloved mother and grandmother--passing away in 1922.

In 1893 Addie graduated from Brodhead high school, delivering a deep and eloquent commencement address. Hannah vowed to somehow raise the money to send Addie to the University of Wisconsin in Madison (30 miles away). Addie spent one day touring the University and concluded that she would miss her mother too much to ever be a career woman. As an alternative, she promptly passed the test which certified her as a grade-school teacher.

Addie secured a teaching position at a country school located about two miles north of Brodhead. She lodged with a farm family across the road from the school. After just three weeks on the job she was overcome with homesickness. She resigned her job, and returned to live with her beloved mother--presumably to "await events." As it turned out, events took 13 years to transpire. Addie's lovely brass hand-held school bell was relegated to the attic, to remain virtually untouched for more than a century.

In 1900 a young Loudon Blackbourne came to Brodhead. He was 21, seeking to make his own way in the world. Typical of the era, he had an eighth-grade education and work experience only in farming. He got a job as a hired hand on a farm outside of Brodhead, and acquired the habit of walking on the railroad track into town on Saturday evenings in search of the mild entertainments then in vogue. The track ran a block from the Smith home, and the first time Loudon saw it he paused and vowed, "I'll make something of myself and have a home like that someday!"

Eventually Addie and Loudon met and they commenced a cautious courtship which centered on the church events and tame parties of the era. In common, they were both of 100 percent English ancestry and both Methodist. It took Loudon years to accumulate the $1,000 in the bank which he felt any responsible young man must possess as a prerequisite to inviting marriage. A thousand dollars then, of course, was the equivalent of three year's income. During a Sunday-afternoon carriage ride, Loudon stopped the horses in the romantic confines of the covered bridge which spanned the Sugar River, and proposed. The couple was married in 1906.

By then Addie was 31 and Loudon was 27. They took up residence, logically enough, with the bride's widowed mother. And, Loudon's vow of "having a home like that someday" was most literally fulfilled. An unkind remark or two in the small-town gossip circles suggested that the ambitious but unskilled young man had married in order to get a house and a store building. From the perspective of early photos, the couple appears to be enjoying the enchantment which accompanies true love.

Addie probably never was described as beautiful, physically. She did, however, have a character which was a virtual duplicate of that of her mother. She was caring, loving, giving, sincere, patient, and kind. It would not be too much of an overstatement to assert that she never made anyone angry in her life. She eagerly sought the stereotypical role which society expected from women in her era, and she graciously spent her life being a faithful and loving wife and mother. Such was Addie's self-less nature that she even opposed the vote for women. She literally believed the Biblical statement that "the husband is the head of the wife," and concluded that women's suffrage would merely give married men two votes, and that would be unfair to single men.

The good news about Loudon Blackbourne was that he had "movie-star" good looks. His facial features were strikingly handsome, he stood six-foot-two, and had very broad shoulders. He was good-natured, loved to associate with people, was scrupulously honest, sincere about his religious faith, and devoted to his family. On the very rarest of occasions he could feel that he'd been pushed too far, and then display a healthy anger.

The harder truth about Loudon was that he had a miserable time finding a vocation. He hated being a farm-hand, which is what he was when he met Addie. With his marriage, remember, did come a store building. Immediately following the honeymoon, the store tenant was turned out and Loudon opened a wallpaper store. Soon he hated it--complained that his store was his prison. He sold out and travelled for several years as a brush salesman. This was not lucrative, and the only good news is that the circumstance generated letters which have become part of this volume.

Giving up the brush business, Loudon tried farming for a year. He lost money at it and sold the farm at a loss. Finally, in 1917 he went to work in the bank in Woodford--some 30 miles west of Brodhead. In the twenties he moved to a slightly larger bank in nearby Argyle and became Cashier. All this time he rented cheap rooms and commuted home on weekends--and generated more letters.

Banking proved to be Loudon's niche. He excelled at it, and it was the only thing he ever excelled at. He needed his banking career to last his lifetime, but life often doesn't care what we mere mortals need. In 1929 the Great Depression came down on people like an avalanche, and Loudon's bank closed. He never was to find another banking job. So, at age 50--and with two girls in college, whose expenses he'd promised to pay--he returned permanently to Brodhead and opened a gas station.

After a decade of marginal income from the gas station, Loudon swallowed what must have been his last ounce of pride, and opened a business in the old store building. What else? A wallpaper store. At age 60 he was doing the same thing in the same place that he'd hated at age 27. Successful at first, the store slowly declined as Loudon's style of merchandising failed to keep pace with the times. He never felt he could retire, and was still operating his store on the day he fell dead at age 84. Loudon had always invested in the stock market. He would never sell stock and enjoy the proceeds, saying, "One can't spend his investment capital!" So, the ambitious man who never had much money to enjoy, left a substantial amount to his heirs.

The Third Generation

The children born to Loudon and Addie were two daughters--Rosamond, born in 1909; and Joyce, born in 1910. The two girls were inseparable friends, even going on to be roommates in college. They lived as idyllic a life as children could in their era. They were bright and did well in school. They wore fashionable clothes, and had the best dolls and toys. By no means spoiled, they were well-adjusted young ladies living in a perfectly humane and loving home environment.

Things change from one generation to the next. Rosamond and Joyce perhaps loved their mother as much as she had loved hers, but somehow they were able to take the big step and go the university in Madison. They even had the same major--Latin. They graduated during the depths of the Depression and each began a slow migration from one school to another around the state of Wisconsin, ever in search of a slightly higher paying teaching job.

Joyce never outgrew a deep homesickness and gave in to it after more than a decade as an independent professional. She secured a teaching job back in Brodhead, and moved into the family home to live with her parents. In 1945--at age 35--she married Arnold Condon. They had gone to the high school prom together 17 years earlier, and had had a none-too-impassioned intermittent relationship ever since. He had dedicated his youthful years to becoming a college professor--and had even stronger ties to his mother than Joyce had to hers.

17

To complete the story of the third generation, Rosamond married a fellow West Allis teacher, John Plichta. They never had children and were frequent weekend and summer visitors to the old family home. They were something of an "extra-special" set of parents and grandparents to Gregg Condon and his sons.

The Fourth Generation

Joyce and Arnold were destined to have trouble from the start. But, they bravely went to Tucson, Arizona where Arnold was named head of the Business Education Department. There a son was born, Gregg--who 51 years later was destined to be the author of this work. Parental ties were strong, relationships complicated, and in a few years Arnold's mother was living with him; and Joyce and son Gregg were back in the family home in Brodhead. And that is how Gregg came to be the fourth generation of his family to live in the family home.

Gregg Condon went to college, and completed bachelor's, master's, and doctor's degrees by age 27. He worked in New York City as editor of the Gregg Shorthand series of textbooks. After securing senior authorship of the textbook series, he became a professor at the University of Wisconsin-Eau Claire.

The Fifth Generation

Addie died in 1949 and Loudon in 1963. After Gregg went to college in 1965, Joyce lived in the home alone. Thirty-some years after Joyce and Arnold had separated, and with the older generation dead, Arnold and Joyce got back together and lived--where else?--in the old family home. Thus Gregg's sons, Scott and Todd, came to know the old family home as "Grandma and Grandpa's house." And, they became the fifth generation of the family to love the home and its traditions.

Ironically, Francis Smith--who built the family home--lived in it for only five years, but his descendants stayed for 120. The letters they left in the attic tell their story and define the times in which they lived.

18

PART TWO

THE STORY THE LETTERS TELL

The story which the letters tell is contained in this portion of the volume. In presenting the letters, the original spelling, capitalization, and punctuation has been maintained. Early writers often used a dash to indicate the end of a sentence, and that practice is repeated here. Where the original writer used no punctuation at the end of a sentence, additional space is left between words to aid the reader in deciphering where one sentence ends and the next begins.

Paragraphing was as uncertain as punctuation in early letters. Some multi-page letters were but a single paragraph. To improve the readability and eye appeal of the letters, paragraph breaks have been interjected at logical points.

Readers who are familiar with handwritten documents from the 1700s will recall the practice of using the letter *f* to express the letter *s* on occasion, particularly to represent the first *s* when the double *s* occurs. This practice is not repeated in this book. The letter *s* is consistently used in order to minimize distraction to the reader.

The letters in this volume have been carefully selected for their content. All of the letters from the 1850s are presented because they reveal so much about life in that now remote time. The letters from the Civil War era represent a selection calculated to make a concise and complete coverage of what the writers had to offer.

Letters from later eras were likewise carefully selected to convey a sense of the story of their times. In these later eras, a very small portion of the collection is presented--just enough to round out the story of five generations whose story the letters tell.

Each letter is preceded by an introduction which sets the scene. Archaic expressions which might baffle the present-day reader are defined in parentheses immediately following the term within the body of the letter.

Francis Smith is pictured in a well-worn tintype photo which dates from the very dawn of photography in the 1850s.

CHAPTER FOUR

THE MOVE WEST, 1853-1859

The decade of the 1850s generated more letters than any other--twice as many, in fact, than the second-most-prolific decade which was the 1940s. For this we can be grateful, as the letters from that now distant decade contain a constant flow of surprises about history, the evolution of the language, and the human drama.

About half the letters from the 1850s were in their original envelopes. None of these bore stamps. Instead, they all had a hand-written note from the postmaster saying, "Paid, 3 cts." Only one envelope had a postal cancellation mark on it, and that entirely illegible. The envelopes were of no standard sizes, but all were smaller than modern envelopes. The smallest--which is pictured in this volume--measures only two by four inches.

Francis Smith and Abigail Davidson, both from Grafton, New York, were married in 1850. Francis was 28 and Abigail was 25, perhaps unusually old ages for marriage at the time. In 1853 they moved from Grafton to Palmyra, New York, and this move generated the first of the letters in the collection. In only a year they were destined to move again--this time to Wisconsin.

The first of the letters, is written a week after Francis and Abigail left their home town. It is written by Abigail's father, Paul K. Davidson. The Deborah mentioned in the closing is Paul's second wife, Abigail's stepmother.

Paul Davidson writes so well--indeed, brilliantly at times. Much of his writing fills this chapter. He was born in the late 1700s. What was his education? Was he self-taught as were many of America's great founders?

March 27, 1853   Grafton, New York

Dear Children

having one hour to Spare after having got ready for church I imbrace the opportunity of conversing with you a few minutes in this Silent manner

We received your letter last by Friday's mail--I was drawing out timbers from Stevens mill and promised to go to the P. O. before I came home but while I was unloding the Second load I Saw Augusta and Maryetta triping down from behind the wood pile and on scaring me she cried out I've got it. I've got it   At the top of her voice----and what was it that She had got? That excited So much Joy? Why a letter from a Sister who had been absent a little more than a week----a time that would not have caused any particular anxiety while she was here with us----

but the Blessings of Social Society and relation as was Said by the poet "Seem to brighten as they take their flight, and now what is it that so tightly binds up the hearts of friends and relatives save but that Spirit which is the evidence of immortality which is continually panting and striving for happiness in the pursuits of life----and causes the parting Sigh, or even the flowing tear" so beautifully expressed in the words of Wordsworth.

But while our feeble natures are properly exercised by the privations of this imperfect state----how inexpressably dear is that hope which is an anchor to the Soul assuring us of a home to which we are all traveling where all the afflictive Scenes of earth will be forever Swallowed up in that rest that remaineth for the people of God   But you will begin to think I have turned preacher----So I will leave the subject which is allways dear to me and talk about other matters

we were glad to hear of your save arrival and about the pleasantness of your new home----I Sincerely wish you much joy in your new situation and that your days, and months, and years may glide Smoothly and hapily through life---and in forming new acquaintences, you may establish a character Such as becomes those professing godliness and be a blessing to Society around you

23

we are all in usual health   Grandmother Slept all night last night for the first time Since She has been sick   She got up feeling verry cheerful this morning and was much pleased with her new calico dress

I have been very busy this week---had sawing 4 days and conveying **(hauling logs)** *two---I Send you a Canton Register dressed in mourning for the death of its Senior editor brother, Asa Lee--who died on the fifth of the present month* **("brother," here means a fellow Christian)**

we expect elder Rogers to day and would wish you here to sing with us but your Singing there and ours here--may unite with the Millioins more and ascend in one song of Gratitude and praise to God for his loving kindness and longsuffering towards us   but my hour is about up---So with you our best wishes   and love to you

we bid you good bye

P K & Deborah Davison

Mary Davidson writes to her sister, Abigail, while she and Francis are living near Palmyra, New York. It is newsy in the extreme, and fraught with Mary's sense of humor. And, the term for *gossip* in the last paragraph, well--read on and find out that one for yourself!

April 3, 1853   Grafton, New York

*dear brother and sis*ter

As I have now A few leisure moments I thought to improve them by writing to you. Now I am going to talk at you and if you happen to be turning your best ear towards old Grafton you may hear something I have to say.

I have some great news to write   Last evening Eliphlet Steward esq united in bands of matrimony Mr Benjamin Hayner and Miss Mercy Allen and if that is not news then I will not write any more to day   Palmer west got to Scuffling with Jim Scrivens while drunk and broke his leg They think it will end his life   We recieved a letter from uncle

24

Rowland yesterday stating the cause of uncle Asa's death with the lung fever but partially recovered when he was taken with a fit of the apoplexy which carried him off.

uncle Rowland says he intends visiting us about the first of June if nothing happens. we are all well as usual   Grandma is a good deal better than she was when you left us   She can call for a fire yet and then for air as well as ever **(she asks for a fire because she is cold, and then as soon as she gets the fire she asks for fresh air because she is too hot)**

I suppose you are making sugar at no small rate   I hope you will remember me while you are eating it. I want you to write if you please all about how you like out there and all about every thing

mother had to go see Mary F week before last   She would be so lonesome now Abigail had gone away   It wasn't any trouble atall **(at all)**   *She is in Scolding trim now I tell you*

Francis I would like to know whither **(whether)** *you Slung Snot* **(gossiped)** *any or not   if you did I will say O no you Shouldnot   I close by sinding love to all   there is a kiss on one corner of this paper   if you can find it you are welcome to it*

your sister

Mary

People in the 1850s benefitted from very little education. There were no compulsory attendance laws. Life was tenuous, and many families felt that they could not afford the luxury of having children in school; all hands were needed for work at home.

The next pair of letters are in Augusta's handwriting. One letter is on her own behalf, and the other letter is one dictated to her by Deborah Davidson. Deborah can neither read nor write. It is an era when some of the most ambitious people--people who take leadership roles in the community--are illiterate.

25

April 3, 1853   Grafton, New York

Dear Sister

I now seat myself to answer your letter that was written so long ago. we received your letter today about ten oclock and was glad to hear from you we are all as well as usual   I was very sorry to know that you was so out of health   I hope you will get well soon and come and see us   I want to see you very much Indeed

I am so large you would not know me **(she is a child who is growing fast)** *I suppose you well remember mrs westervelt   She has got 2 very nice little girls   They are as prety as little dolls   franks folks have a very nice baby   It can sit alone*

you should see father driving our team now   We have got a very nice span of horses   I dont believe we will go to town atall   I feel as though it was not Sunday as I have not been to church   I was weighed when I was to uncle charles store   you cannot guess how much I weighed   I weighed 106 lbs and I think that was pretty well for me

I guess I will close as I have gotto write a few lines for ma   so good bye from A **(Augusta)** *Davidson*

Dear Daughter

as your father and augusta have been a writing to you I thought I would write a few lines to you   it is now Tuesday morning and it is very cold it has been snowing here   My health is pretty good now so that I do all my hard work myself

I was very sorry to hear that your health was so poor   I hope your health will be better soon   perhaps it would be bad for your health to travel I would like to have you come very much but if you do not I guess your father will come out there if he possibly can

your father sometimes talks of going to Troy **(moving to Troy, New York)** *but I do not want to go because we have such good meetings*

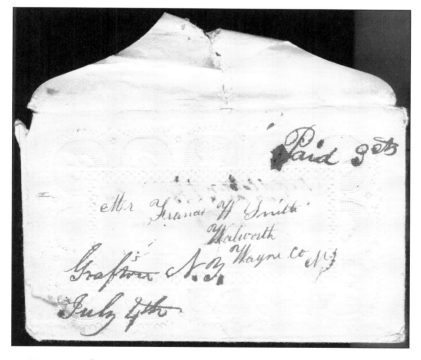

These two envelopes typify those used in the 1850s. The smallest measures only two by four inches. The handwriting is so dainty that one wonders how the postal workers managed to read it.

(church services) here   I wish you could be here and heare some of mr
baldwins sermons   You would be very much please about them

so no more at present from you Dearest beloved mother   D Davidson

The following two letters were written on the same page. The large sheet of paper containing the letters measures 12 by 15 inches, and it is evident that it was torn from a larger sheet. The paper of all the letters of the 1850s is of non-standard sizes, just as are the envelopes. The paper of these letters has light blue lines printed on it and the spacing of these lines conforms to the rulings of modern notebook paper.

The first letter is to Francis and Abigail from Abigail's sister, Mary J. Davidson. The author of this letter is a teacher, and yet she follows almost none of the present-day rules of punctuation, capitalization, and paragraphing. Application of standard English rules begins in this collection of letters with people who were educated in the 1890s.

The second letter is from Abigail's father, Paul Davidson.

May 8, 1853   Grafton, New York

Dear sister

as it falls to me to do all the writing I will attempt it again. We are all well, and hope these few lines will find you enjoying the same. We have A rainy Sunday to day and it seems very lonesome but I think if I could go over to Abigail's it would not be quite so bad. But, that I cannot do and so I have to content myself the best way I can. I have not been into your house since the morning you left nor do I wish to.

I commenced my School last monday and like it very well. Boarded to Mr. Worthingtons. So I am one week nearer seeing you than I was last week pa wants to write to Francis about his wagon which he said he wanted him to send as soon as he could and so I must hurry as it is getting quite late and give him A chance

uncle Jake's folks have gone   went a fortnight ago last Friday. Franklin carried **(gave them a ride)** *to Troy and when they got about A half A mile beyond Millville he turned out to go by A team and Ady fell out   and the hind wheel run over her back and they thought She was hurt pretty bad their baby went very well   it only had one crying spell from here to Troy and two from there to where they went*

we had a letter from them yesterday   they said Ady was not hurt as bad as they thought she was.   and that Andrew cried very often to go home so he could go to aunt ep's to get some milk and Jonnycake.

I said our folks were all well   they are all well excepting grandma, and she has got so she dont know anything scarcely   She falls out of her chair and they have to watch her most all of the time but I must stop so no more

Mary P. Davison

Dear Children

I write a few words in Sister marys letter to inform you of our Good health and more than merited blessings. our Spring has been pretty plesant So far though not verry forward **(the season is arriving late)** *we have today a rather cold rain--and sleepy Sunday with   no meeting* **(no church service)**

I carried **(drove)** *your waggon and box to Troy Last Wenesday   the Receipt for which I inclose and Send you   I should have written Sooner but the agent Said he could not Send it 'till the last of the week. So I though that a line today would reach you as quick as the waggon would get to Palmyra*

Day after tomorrow I have to attend an extra meeting of the board of Supervisors at Troy----Grandmother is verry troublesome and unwell does not pretend to lie on the bed at all   P K Davison

29

This letter is from **Paul Davidson** to his daughter **Abigail** and her husband **Francis**. He says it is written "according to contract," meaning to keep his promise to write. The letter is written after Paul has journeyed by train from Troy to Palmyra and return. The railroad line is new in 1853 and Paul reports at length on the wonders of his first train trip.

Consider the scenario. Here is a man born in the 1700s, and now in late middle age he encounters his first train. Advancing technology still captures the attention of people; but when the rate of technological change was extremely slow, its impact must have been all the more dramatic.

June 30, 1853   Grafton, New York

Dear Children

according to contract I sit down this morning to inform you of my Safe arrival at home about nine o. k. P.M. of the Same day I left you and had the pleasure of finding all well----Franklin had not got the Small pox--nor was mother any worse than wen I left home----Augusta was Sitting up to wait till pa come home and was hanging around my neck before I was fairly into the house

Mary came home from her School the next night to See me and hear from you   She appears verry healthy for her and is making every calculation to come out and see you the last of August   Asa and 'gusta thought a great deal of their apples and Hector carries those peaches in his pocket to show them to the boys

I am interrogated by every one I see almost in relation to your country and whether Abigail is contented or not   We did not stop at all the places on the way. but Stoped at Lyons and Clyde two vilages nearly as large as Palmyra--having depos out one side about as far as at Palmyra **(the railroad stations at these towns are located similarly to that of Palmyra)**

We arrived at Syracuse at 20 minutes past 10. and staid 'till ll ocklock----it rained continually all the while So that I had no chance to see the place except from the depo but judging from what I could See I Should think it was a much larger place than I supposed it was----Some of its taverns would answer well for kings pallaces and Queen Vic. **(Queen Victoria of England)** *and Prince Albert themselves might well be contented if they were well naturalized in this country and owned the Syracuse House*

Uncle Milton came one train ahead of me and arrived in Troy 1/2 hour first   I have not seen him----consequently I dont know how he found the folks **(meaning their condition)** *at canadilla*

I found my plantation **(literally meaning where he had planted things; not meaning a palatial estate)** *looking as well as I expected. my patches of corn looked as large as common in the west and pumkins, squashes, and cucumbers--better*

we are engaged now hoeing potatoes and shall nearly get through to day with what are long enough **(he is tired of hoeing potatoes)**----*straw berries are very plenty this summer   plese write soon and tell us all about it.*

Yours P. K. Davison

This letter is to Abigail Smith from her sister Mary P. Davidson. It is written on the 77th anniversary of Independence Day, but only scant reference is made to the fact. Later letters in this chapter wax eloquently patriotic, but Mary is content with small-talk on this occasion.

Research did not find definitive information as to what a "quill popgun" was. Mary's letter is delightfully flippant in regard to her ex-boyfriend, and her attitude might well be a product of the 1990s rather than the 1850s.

July 4, 1853   Grafton, New York

Dear sister.

it is with pleasure I seat myself to write to you. I would mak a few excuses for not writing before but knowing you will not care about hearing them   I will tell you what I have to tell and let it go promising not to do so again. I am in hopes I shall not have to write many more letters before I have the pleasure of seeing you. if nothing happens I shall be there in about four weeks and then I think you will get one kissing and tell Francis he to too shal have that kiss.

to day is the 4th and they are going it hot and heavy   my dear little Alva **(sarcastic reference to her ex-boyfriend)** *is going, he went to Troy Saturday to the livery stable and hired him a horse and carriage and is agoing to carry hannah Scullen   now you see if I havnt broken his heart so that he couldnot eat any thing but lemon pie for six weeks, I could have went to* **(too)**   *now I begin to see where I missed it   but it is to late to repent now--as there is no mushy for me as pa said* **(delightful slang for "romance")**

Ben Hayner and Mercy Allen was married. Asa is in a great hurry to go to the center **(what we might call "downtown" Troy)** *and as he is going to carry this to the office* **(Post Office)** *I must hurry   he has got him A quill popgun and is going to hold the fourth* **(celebrate July 4)**

I could write A great deal more but have not time so no more at present---I will write again before I come. To dear sister   good bye   from your sister   Mary P. Davison

Here is another letter from Mary P. Davidson. Rather than write to her sister, Abigail, this time; she is writing to Abigail's husband, Francis. Mary is clearly miffed that Abigail has not answered her letters and makes that point--well--most pointedly! One hallmark of the letters from the 1850s is that they are very unabashed in revealing emotion. Both positive and negative sentiments are presented full force without the mitigating influences of pride or tact.

Mary's readers understood her in the context of their times, and they knew the extent to which she was bluntly showing anger and the extent to which she was overstating her case for the sake of humor. These interpretations are now lost in the mists of a century and a half.

August 21, 1853   Grafton, New York

Dear brother **(actually brother-in-law)**

I take my seat again to write a few lines to you. It is a long time since we heard from you and we begin to think you have forgotten all about the folks in the old state. I have written to Mrs. Smith **(Abigail)** *I don't know how many times but she dont think it necessary to answer or does not have time or something   I dont know what. But suffice to say we dont hear from you so I thought to write to you for I shant* **(contraction of "shall not")** *write to her again until she answers so she may set that down* **(officially record it)** *you tell her so if you please.*

I told her when I wrote last that I would write again the next Sunday and let you know when I was coming, but I was taken sick and was sick about a fortnight and so I did not write but it would have done no good if I had for the Davisons are vary slow folks and it takes them a great while to make up their minds   I did not know untill to day when I should come and dont hardly know now uncle Milton calculates to start **(travel to Palmyra, New York)** *next Monday one week from tomorrow if nothing happens. but it will be rather doubtful about my coming then   but I will wait aspell* **(awhile)** *and tell you by and by*

Monday Morning August 22, 1853

I will now try to finish my letter   grandma is hollowing **(hollering)** *like a good fellow for a fire. she says the folks will have it in print before long that Deacon Davison has froze his poor old mother to death. and mother thinks Miss Prude* **(Mary's reference to herself)** *might as well help get breakfast as to be a writing all the time.*

but now I will tell you when I am a coming if nothing happens   I shall be there two weeks from today, and pa says he wants you to lay yourself out on the platform at the depot for a sign **(so they can recognize him)** *and look out for the engine when the bell rings.   now I want you to remember two weeks from today,   if you can read this you will do well and I guess their will be no mistakes nor bruises and I dont want you to eat up all the peaches.* **(Mary hopes to visit them, and would like to have some of their good New York peaches left.)**

33

if their **(there)** *is a letter comes there to the Post-Office take it out and read it to your hearts content   but I must stop writing as I have told all the news   only that Thomas Brown is married to the Mary Jane McChesney the girl that used to work to* **(at)** *the tavern   so no more*

good bye   Mary P. Davison

Paul Davidson again addresses his daughter and son-in-law as "children." In these early times when agriculture was the livelihood, roads were dirt and transportation by foot or animal, and heat was only from a fire, a lot of attention was given to the weather. Likewise, health was an almost constant topic in these times when good health was never taken for granted. In the midst of the routine news of the day, Paul turns to his most cherished topic, his deep religious faith.

September 18, 1853   Grafton, New York

Dear Children

I sit down this evening to write a few lines to inform you of our health which is about as good as usual. mother **(*his* mother)** *is rather declining for a few days past and is almost entirely helpless*

we have had a verry wet time for a few days past but to day has been verry warm and pleasurable   we had a little frost last monday which has done no dammage as my crops were all out of the way **(harvested)**

We had a good sermon to day from Hebrews 11 v 14 "For those that say such things xc" **(etc.)**   *our singing has become rather scattered which with Some other things makes me almost sick of home----and wish the time to come "When I could in His earthly courts be standing with my beloved ones at home"* **(receive God's final judgment here on Earth and be taken to Heaven).**

but All things Shall work together for good to those who are in Christ Jesus who are the called according to his purpose. So let us with cheerfulness pursue our pilgramage journey keeping the end in view----

Joseph and his wife are here to night and quite a number of the neighboring young folk, I want you to write often and let me know all about the crops I want a Specimen of Francis hand writing telling all of the prospects of the farm xc. **(etc.)**

I have traded off my horses with Amos B Sweet for his Oxen and 90 dollars calling it 200 dollars in all----Oxen and other stock are verry high! **(high priced)** *hay is worth from 15 to 18 dollars per ton in Troy the potatoe crop is tight all over this part and Some pieces* **(fields)** *beginning to rot the rust killed the vines generally before they were more than half grown I leave the other page for the boys but cant git after them to write*

yours with best wishes P. K. Davison

Paul Davidson writes to Abigail and Francis from the offices of the County Supervisor (he is a member of the Board). He then expresses at great length, and with tremendous sensitivity, that he misses his daughter who has moved away. This letter certainly dispels any stereotype of American men of the era as being gruff and taciturn.

November 23, 1853 Troy, New York

Dear Children

While Sitting leisurely by the table in the Supervision room thinking of home and the affairs pertaining thereto I recollected a little matter of tax that was overcharged last year and looking around I found a sheet of paper and wrote a Short resolution to introduce upon the subject and after cutting it off **(the common cost-conscious practice of cutting off and saving the portion of a page not used)** *I Sat musing and hearing the chat of those around me when all at once my imagination ran up River Street to the upper railroad office where I Saw in my imagination my affectionate children Just on the point of Starting for the <u>West</u>, with bag and baggage----striving to suppress the feelings which unavoidably aggitate our souls when we part from the home of our childhood and the scenes which we have cherished from our earliest recollection in all of* *this she succeeded very well till the significant ding--ding--of the bell and the "all a board" of the conductor announced that the time of parting had come and the strong feeling of natural affection found relief in a parting kiss and of an effusion of tears*

the next minute the cars **(train)** *were gone and I found myself slowly pacing the walk toward Congress Street with the Scenes of life through which I had passed flitting through my mind   and the Scenes of Sorrow and of Joy through which we had passed together came so suddenly upon me in spite of my efforts to suppress it*

feeling again found relief in tears which I dashed away as soon as possible lest the busy crowd observe me----but my tears were not those of Sorrow but the result of a feeling which cannot be described. and may not be imagined except by those who have been circumstanced in life as we have been.

a kind of unearthly Joy came to my relief in the contemplation that that daughter loved her father with a love entirely beyound the comprehension of the crowd who saw her weep in the cars and which shall only be complete when our broken family Shall be reunited beyonned the reach of Sorrow, or a possibility of a separation in the mansions of eternal rest---- and with a sincere wish for her and her husbands safety and prosperity I found myself under Allens Shed looking after my team which I found in good order and was soon under way for old grafton where I had left what remained of my earthly treasure, and had to answer all the questions which ma, and Franklin and Mary and Hector and 'gusta had to ask about Francis and Abigails Starting **(leaving).**

Asa Phillips is at my house----he Sawed his thumb and laid himself up for the present some two weeks ago, and came up to Grafton   Got up a petition to the collector of the port of New York Got all the big Softs **(the well-to-do)** *in Bambusucry Troy to sign it and went back to New York to try to get an appointment of night watch in the custom house----left his petition and has not yet herd from it yet----but will not probably succeed. if he doesnt succeed he talks some of going into the ice business next spring*

Some changes have come over us since you left----Mother has Gone to her rest for which She So earnestly prayed so long, and of course makes a large blank in our circle and care, and we believe is now in the presence of him whom She So much loved and followed through evil as well as through good report and has received the reward of him who said "be thou faithful unto death and I will give unto thee a crown of life"----Betsy Hydorn watched with her the night before She died----and about a week or ten days after was taken violently with the collick and died in a few days----old mister Jonathan Brock died five or Six weeks ago and also Wm. P Phillips' wife a week or two after

well now you are settled in your new home which I have had the satisfaction to see, and have got my sprightly singing Mary out there with you, who by the bye I commend to your special care while she remains with you

Franklin and my self left home last monday morning about Sunrise for Troy and left the folks all well as usual   but it was So mudy **(muddy)** *and rainy that no one was coming to Troy So we paddled* **(humorous expression meaning that they were walking in much water and mud)** *in to quackenkill and waited for the petersburgh Stage about two hours when we concluded to start on foot and before we got to Budsaw* **(?)** *we were overtaken by Enoch Brown with a horse & wagon which he wanted to send to Troy and would be much obliged if we would get in and drive it down for him. So we of course consented and called it one of the times when fortune favours the brave*

but you will ask what was Franklin coming to Troy for? I'll tell you--he has a notion to clerk it here in a grocery and has partly agreed to work for Mr. Adams, where Dexter used to keep **(used to be a storekeeper).**

yours affectionately

P K Davison

This last letter from 1853 provides us with a rare and moving description of the Worlds' Fair then in progress in New York City. The letter is so eloquent at times that it sounds as if it might be quoting from the fair's exhibits, but the words are original to the writer. The sentiments about God and country reveal this common man's conviction that as an American he is part of the most noble effort in the history of civilization. It is the same dedication Lincoln expressed a decade later when he called America, "the last best hope of Earth."

While Paul Davidson is visiting the fair, another citizen of Grafton is working there. She is 17-year-old Hannah Allen, and destined to become Francis Smith's second wife. She has saved a souvenir from the fair. Fifteen years later she will place this souvenir on the mantle of the parlor fireplace in Brodhead, Wisconsin and there it will remain for the next 120 years.

November 27, 1853   Grafton, New York

Dear Children

I am coming to sit down with you **(meaning his letter is taking the place of the face-to-face visit which he would have preferred)** *to tell you all about the Fair, and you Shall agree not to be grammarizing or making derision if I speak Somewhat at ramblance* **(perhaps he coined this word meaning he might ramble)** *for it is said that writing to a friend is nothing but thinking aloud*

I had a strong invitation to accompany some of our Supervisors to New York Some Six weeks ago which I accepted   and we Started at about 8 with mostly rough and mountainous scenry passing through the eastern part of Columbia Dutchess putman and Westchester passing no village of any amount after we left Strattinson four corners till we came to mornsina about twelves miles this side of New York which is a butiful village Said to have been founded by Governor Morris of Connecticut

just below this we crossed a verry high bridge over the Spiten Dovla which unites Manhattan--the island on which New York is built--with the main land   while crossing we were Some 15 ft above the telegraph wire

38

and so nigh (**near**) *the edge that we could not See the bridge under us without putting our heads out of the window----but we had no fault to find as long as it carried us safe over----here we began to see large country residences which gave us to understand that we were nearing some large city* (**the location is now a great many miles within the city**).

After a time we enter'd a tunnel and all was Darkness, except once in a few rods we could see a light spot on the side by and by the light of day again burst upon us and we found ourselves in the midst of the great city and securing lodging at the <u>clairemont house</u> we proceded to visit the fair in a "mule car"--drawn by horses

we entered the fair on the west side where after giving up our tickets we were requested to give up our canes, umbrellas or what ever we might have to walk with. they were deposited in a kind of rack standing about a foot and a half high on the floor being divided into checks 2 1/2 inches Square--each check being numbered--and each of us received a Small check of paper corresponding in number with that on the rack which contained our property

this ceremony over we paced around and the Great world's fair was in full view before us (**In the next sentence Paul attempts to write very conversationally by imagining a request for further information from one of the people to whom he is actually writing.**) *and here comes up the request from sister Mary for Pa to tell her what he Saw at the worlds fair a task which would require a number of Sheets of paper like this---- but I will Try and tell Something about Some things that we noticed in our short stay, for although we were there 8 hours we could hardly glance at all the articles which represented the taste and individuality of the different nations of the earth*

The first and all-absorbing object that Struck our gaze was the great guiding star of our liberty and liberal institutions, Washington on horseback Standing on a platform in the center of this vast show room, perhaps four times as large as life with hat in hand and raised in his stirups as if to say.. welcome Englishman, Frenchman, Italian, Russian, German, or what nation soveren (**sovereign**) *under the Whole Heaven you may chance to represent welcome to our holmes, our hospitality and the* *enjoyment of our institutions   You may have full liberty to mingle with our people and think and act as best suits your conscience   provided in so thinking or acting you do nothing to interfere with the rights and privileges of others, for here we hold all men to be <u>Free and equal</u> and make no distinction except by merits alone*

and if you chance to think our liberties the best article exhibited here and wish when the fair is over to purchase the article for your own use you are welcome to as large a Share was you wish for by ownly **(only)** *declaring your intention of becoming an American citizen and if you wish for further information upon the Subject at any time, I refer you to my friend Daniel Webster who Stands behind me on the next platform, of whom you have all heard, and who for your convenience has brought our constitution with him--and as if affraid some spy from the old world might have an evil design upon it, Stands with one hand resting upon the ponderous volume and the other upraised as if to explain or defend it.*

After Spending a short time inspecting the Statuary and bronze figures in the center of the first floor our attention was turned to the galleries of the Structure which was of itself a great curiosity with flights of stairs leading up on almost every side and divided into apartments for the convenience of the principle nations represented here and labeled in large letters <u>United States</u>--<u>Great Britain</u>--<u>France</u>--<u>Germany</u> &c. &c **(etc.)** *we ascended the Stairs leading to the department of the united States--where were collected Specimens of the various manufacturers of our country from the tea sets of massive gold down to the Self-rocking cradle and baby jumper----also articles of finest manufacture in Silks, Shawls, Carpeting, broad cloth, cutlery and farming utensils, clocks, watches &c. &c.----*

after wandering through the various apartments and reading the instructions and warnings to visitors to keep "hands off" and seeing the full grown and full Dressed American lady as she Stood in her house of Glass Slowly turning as if wishing to exhibit her fine form and fashionable dress to the best possible advantage--we craped **(crept)** *over to Canada-- and then to England--France, and in short, all the principle countries of the old world where we saw nearly the Same things with only the variation Suited to the varied taste and climate they represented* *after wandering and gazing till we were tired--hardly noticing that the Scene had changed from Day to Gass light--we came round to the head of one of its principle staircases and found ourselves in full view of the greatest and most wonderful Sight we had yet witnessed--the Pallace itself with beautiful Chandeliers and thousands of gass lights in full blaze of light Showing off the whole Structure of the building with its thousands of visitors continually rushing and moving about to the best possible advantage*

as we Stood looking and admiring the fairy Scene around us, one of our company remarked that if he Should awake from Sleep and find himself in a place like that he Should think himself in heaven----This remark Seemed to break the enchantment into which my mind had fallen and I began to contrast in my imagination this masterly work of art with that Heaven toward which my hopes had so long tended--I found that to a believing mind the comparison sinks into entire insignificance----for instead of having a City of inconceivable Size with Streets of gold and golden gates set in perls with no night there but the "Lord God and the Lamb being the light of the city" we were surrounded with a building of nothing but Iron, Glass, and wood and lighted with gass----here were people of nearly all tongues and nations differing in dress and manners attended with numerous police with clubs in hand to keep order and prevent crime---- There will be an innumerable company composed of every nation under heaven, whose language, appearance, and dress, shall all be alike having been redeemed and having washed their robes and made them white in the blood of the lamb----where nothing that is sinful or unclean Shall ever be permitted to enter----and hunger and thirst, pain and sickness, and the thousand anxieties which so often destroy our enjoyment here Shall be known no more for ever

looking around I saw the backside of one of our company just going out of sight through a door some 20 or 30 feet from me and hastening to join them I found we had entered the Picture Gallery a chamber apart from the rest about 200 ft long 20 ft wide and 20 or 25 ft high--completely Seiled on evry side with the choicest specimens of painting arranged in three rows one above the other--the largest at the bottom and all numbered and visitors furnished with a book containing corresponding numbers again while the drawing was explained and the name and the country of the author given----this room was lighted by two large gass pipes running overhead through its whole length and burners about 4 inches apart and said to be about 1200 in number----and here I must stop for want of room and as I have not time to review my letter you will be obliged to receive it mistakes and all. and if there is any of it you cannot read I will explain it when I see you and so with my best wishes I bid you

good-bye from your father

P K. Davison

In this letter, Abigail receives a letter from her older brother, Thomas Franklin Davidson, who lives in Troy. In this letter, as in so many from the era, reference is made to church service being held Sunday evening. Members of the family had no consistent spelling of their surname; sometimes they spelled it with a second *d*, sometimes without.

January 1, 1854 Troy, New York

Dear Sister Abigail

As i have been looking over the last lines that you Wrote me i have given up going to church this after Noon i thought i Would Write you a few lines. You wrote that you was very much disappointed because i did not come out there this fall. you want **(a further contraction of the word *wasn't*)** *any more disappointed than i Was.*

but i have but a Small Space here So i must write what you wanted me to. you Wanted i Should write what kind of a Store i was in **(working in)** *i am in a drygood and grocery Store and the price* **(wages)** *and particulars i Stated in Marys letter. A D P* **(Asa Davison)** *has gone back N York Some time ago*

i didnt receive your letter untill fryday Evening. it was advertised and there Was Something curious about it i think i have called for it now for Sometime but it was advertised before i could get it **(There was no home**

42

delivery of mail; everyone "called for it" at the Post Office. The Post Office would publish, or advertise, the names of people who had mail waiting for them.)

tell Francis to Write as Soon as he can and Write What he is up to   next and all about it   i Want you to check up   and the next letter you write me Write Something to cheer me up   i Shall be out there in less than Six or Eight months i think if nothing happens.

i am a getting acquainted With Some of the folks about **(around)** *here and i go to church and feel more contented than i did   i like the business that i am in very well   and, about my head--i can carry it as high as any of them*

there is one thing i must tell you if i have got room   i went up to grafton last Saturday night and Sunday afternoon i went down to fosters as a matter of course   you know   well it was good Sleighing   i had my little colt **(euphemism for his girlfriend, Jane)** *along   got down there a little before dark and talked it over a Spell and thought it would be a fine notion to go to church. So we went up and walked in to church to gather* **(together)** *and Sat to gather   and if there Want* **(wasn't)** *a Staring there then i dont know anything about it.*

Jane is the prettiest girl that there is in grafton quite a compliment for her but you may keep it to your Self. oh there is one more thing i like to forget **(likely to forget)**. *Pa has bought 2 Lots in troy and if nothing happens will be Living here before a great while. it is most church* **(nearly time for church)** *may be i will go after all*

from you Afectionate Brother Thos. F. Davison

Wal **(well)** *now i Shall have to bid you good bye*

from your affectionate brother T. F. Davison

(Yes, many letter closings in the nineteenth century were remarkably redundant.)

This letter and the next to Abigail consists of one page from brother Asa, and a page from their father, Paul. Note that a new dress has been purchased, and then the price given *per yard*; i.e. they bought cloth which will have to be *made* into a dress. And, note the price. The United States has had its system of money for seventy-some years at this point, and still a child is quoting a price in the English term *pence*. More specifically, the price is "six and six pence." This is verbal shorthand meaning "six shillings and six pence." There are 12 pence to a shilling, and 20 shillings to the English pound.

January 5, 1854   Grafton, New York

Dear Sister

I now take an opportunity of writing a few lines to you. I have been to church to day   Mr Shirley preached   they talk of hiring him. I go to school this winter & study geography arithmetic grammar & writing. i have been through the arithmetic once and part way through again **(repetition was part of teaching methodology in a one-room school where there was one teacher and students representing eight grades).**

Pa & Ma went to troy last week & ma bought her a new dress   it was 6 & 6 pence a yard.

franklin is to home to day   he has harnessed up his colt to day & has taken a ride   he has not been home before since christmas

i *went to troy last fall & staid 2 days   i went around a good deal with pa, but i believe i wrote about that in my letter to Abagail   Joseph has gone to keeping house* **(living independently)** *in the north room   he has bought him a team & talkes of living to* **(in)** *troy next summer. We have sold the home farm to Joel Wager and are going to draw writings* **(write up a contract)** *to morrow   he gives us the privelege of living here another year, the sawmill a year, & the cheese house   he gives us $1,000 for the place*

we will take the cheese house to troy   **(Moving buildings was perhaps more common then than now, in spite of a lack of machinery.)**

Aunt patty is here And Augusta is singing & they both make so much noise that i dont know hardly what i am about

Good Bye

from your Brother Asa

Dear Children--

I imbrace the opportunity of writing you a few lines on the back of this letter to let you know that I have not forgotton you.

we have had a verry open winter **(little snow)** *which has been verry bad for me to get away stuff to get money* **(several inches of snow was needed for a sleigh to haul logs to a sawmill)** *It is now Snowing and we hope it will soon be sleighing*

Oh! if I could have had you two with me to help sing in church today --I loath the Idea of singing in meeting with half smothered voice -- as though the goodness & mercy of God did not demand our whole heart, and voice and Soul united in a song of praise and gratitude uttered in the spirit of complete understanding

we had a Sermon to day by mr. Sherley from Hamilton who is visiting us with an idea of engaging here for the year to come as our preacher.

Franklin is at home to day on a visit   seems well pleased with his place & business in Troy

I talk of Selling out this place with the privilege of living in the house a year   I want to know what you think of the move I talk of making----that is of selling this and building a Small house on the lots I have bargained for in Troy and living there----that would leave me all my wood and timber which I could turn as well living there as here----and have enough of grafton land to cut hay and raise potatoes on for my own use and some to spare

45

if I go to troy my notion would be to keep a little wood and lumber yard on the hill which could be done on the lots I have bought   my lots are on the corner of Farm and 11th Street about 20 rods north of the Methodist meeting house----David Worthington and Ira B Ford have bought lots adjoining and are going to build there next Spring

P K Davison

Abigail's brother, Thomas F., writes again--this time to his brother-in-law, Francis. Actually, the letter is written on behalf of Francis' brother, John. If the reader has grown accustomed to the gentleness and civility of previous letters, major surprises are in store in the brief note which follows.

January 25, 1854   Troy, New York

Francis Smith

As We have commenced an inventory this morning i cant Write but a few words   but What i Was a going to Say John Smith Was here yesterday and he wanted me to write you this morning

John is a going to Start for California the first of next month and he wants you to take his boy Dan **(this is the fifth year of the gold rush)**

he and his Wife has parted   he Says She is a poor Drunken Dam bich and he wont Stand it any longer   he Shall go to California if the boy goes to the Devel **(if here isn't conditional; he means *even if*. *Devel* of course means *devil*, or in modern language, *go to hell*)**

he Says you may take him **(Dan)** *on any Condition that you want to   that you may have him as an adopted Son or in any way you want him   he says he had rather* **(would rather)** *you would have him than any body 'Else* *he wants you to write an answer to this as quick as you receive this   he is going to be around here again the first of the Week   he says if you want Dan he Says he will bring him out there and give him to you*

Yours Respectfully   Thos. F Davison

i want you All too Write as fast as you can   you cant Write them any to fast

This brief letter from Paul Davidson chronicles the completion of the new railroad station in Troy.

February 25, 1854   Troy, New York

Dear Children

I embrace a few brief moments to write some lines to inform you that we are all well or were last monday morning when I left home.   I came here to assist in canvassing the votes given in this county at the late Special Election when we also organized as a board of supervisors and are not yet through

I have had some considerable anxiety for your health and was glad to hear that you are well   we have had a very open winter **(little snow)** *and i have not been able to do much in the woods to advantage   the weather changes about once a week from a south thaw and rain to an extreme <u>Nova Zembla</u>, but no snow*

Yesterday we had a celebration of Washingtons birth day -- about two oclock our attention was attracted by the musick of the military and the booming of the cannon on the hill above 8th Street   and in following up we found that the hall in the new Depot was the place appointed for the ceremonies of the day   in a few minutes all eyes were turned towards the tunnel which goes under Congress and ferry Streets just above congress hall -- when out came the big iron horse -- whistling and smoking as if Aetna or vesuvius **(volcanoes which destroyed cities in ancient times)** *were giving warning to the vilages below of an approching eruption --*

47

Draging a train of 5 or 6 large passenger cars loaded with both branches of the legislator and other invited guests from Albany who came up by invitation to christen the new Union Depot -- a building Said to be one of the largest if not the largest -- of the kind in the united States   it is 800 ft long and 400 wide and cost 200,000 dollars -- the speeches and toasts will probably be published

i must be off to deal with the anxiety and distress of other maters
(This quite thoroughly dispels the ideal notion that earlier and simpler times were free from stress and anxiety.)

your loving father

PK Davison

Once again in this letter, two people have each written a page. This is a typical practice of the era. The letter is to Francis and Abigail. The first page is from Mary, the daughter of Francis' married sister, Rachel Burdick.   The second letter is from Rachel.   People mentioned in the letter who have gone to the "western wilds" are brothers of Francis and Rachel, and the "wild place" they have gone is Wisconsin.

March 11, 1854   Grafton, New York

Dear affectionate Uncle & Aunt

At this late hour I commence to answer your letter   I am almost ashamed of myself that I have not written before but I have been waiting for Ma until I see I have got to commence or you would never get your answer for it is the hardest work for her to write of any one I ever saw

but yours is not the only one that is not answered   I received a letter from Marilla one from Almon & one from Jane a few days ago & one from Aunt Minerva   they all wrote they were well & enjoy themselves   well in the western wilds   I dont feel much like writing to day for I set up with a corpse last night & I did not come away till noon to day so if I make any more mistakes than common you must allow the one I set up with was John Maddison's wife   they live in the widdow Leonards house just this side of there   she has been sick all winter with the consumption & I suppose she has suffered a great deal with poverty as well as pain   & that is not all   John used her very mean just as he always did **(he was always an abusive husband)**

her funeral was to day at the Methodist church.   He is going to break up house keeping & put the children out **(find other people for the children to live with)**

I have told you of the deaths now I must tell you of the marriages.   there was three weddings last sunday   the first one was in the morning   it was George Feather to Sally Denham all of Grafton   John Bonesteel & Melissa Dunham stood up with them   they come to meeting sunday evening as bride and bridesmaid should with white dresses on   woolen shawls & worsted hats & after they had been there a spell, George and tother **(contraction of *the other*)** *fellow come   is that the way they do down there?   The next couple was little John Steward to a girl over in Wms Town   he calls her Lindy Blue*

The third couple was Henry Bonesteel to Louisa Burdick   she has made out to get married   her man lives near the school house where I taught last summer   he is a widdower with 3 children & worth considerable property   I happened to that wedding   I called in **(stopped by)** *from meeting* **(church)** *& she wanted me to stay   I don't know what I shall do   they are taking them all away* **(other girls are marrying all the available bachelors)** *I guess I shall have to come down there and get one* **(a husband)** *you watch a good chance for me.* **(She is showing her sense of humor.)**

But I will stop writing such foolishness & write something of more importance   it is very pleasant here to day   there is no sleighing   there is some snow in places but not enough to do any good   there will be a meeting to night   I think I shall go   Dan has been out & got some gum

& is going to send it if he can   there don't much news transpire around here   I will close my letter now. Aunt Abbagail for your sake and for my sake dont let any one see this letter   write soon as you receive this & I will not wait for Ma & then have to write myself but I will do it in the beginning.

From your affectionate neice

Mary Burdick

Dear Brother and Sister

I now Seat my self to answer your letter after So long a time   we ar all well at present and I hope this mae find you the same   we have had a cold winter some of the coldest wether the people thinks we have had in a great meny years   it is hard times hear but not only hear   wood is vary low now   we have slaying now   from the house to the turnpike the road is even with the weals   it has been so two weaks or more

Jeremiah has driven sixty or seventy logs to the mill   we have snow a nough to draw out wood and logs but not much slaying to Troy   Last summer Jeremiah and Daniel soad a peace **(sewed a field)** *of oats and planted a peace of potatoes   did no more then they commonly did   it is the Same old thing and ever will be*

Nathan is not maried yet but he does not go to petersburgh so often is he did for Sary an comes hear and Stops to three weaks to time   She is hear now   I cannot think why tha do not have the not tide **(knot tied)** *I think it would be best*

I have not wrote to Mary about Daniel **(the same boy who was offered to Francis in an earlier letter)** *Nathan and the rest discouredg me from writing for they thought he warnot such a boy as youd want and thought he would be more dumey* **(dummy)** *then prophet and I did not know of eny one that he could come with* **(she doesn't know of anyone he can live with)** *John Scriven Set out for Ilanois a weak a go and if I had a little place and a house to live in I would start to*

50

if there is a good chance for me write   I received a letter from Manny Humes She wants me to come there but I think I had rather come thare of any whare   I do not now how things will turn yet   I waite patient to now we have an exhibition **(a group-participation church service)** *a weak from next fryday   after that is over I think then Mary will be to home part of the time   She has ben home with Mary D Lucrtia Hidorn Charlott Phillips Lois Wait and to Calvin Stevens.*

Mary Says that She wated for me to write   I have had no such chance to write you can see nor Mary neather for She went school days and went home with the girls night So I think she would not wrote any Sooner   I must Stop writing for youI think it is not worth reding   you must forgive me in bad writing and Splling   my pen is poor   I cannot write with it and I am in Such a herry   You See my pen gives plenty of ink part of the time you wanted me to write   what John was doing he did not write   I have not heard from him   Since this will worry your patient **(try your patience)** *So no more*

good by

Rachel Burdick

Mary Davidson writes to sister Abigail. She describes a church "exhibition." Although this book has revealed but a handful of letters to this point, it should already be evident that the writers had only two main activities in life--work and church, and only two main concerns--health and the weather.

What should be of special intrigue to the reader is the extent to which the church is the focal point of community life. By contrast, school is a minor institution having no extracurricular activities and few students left by the time they are in their teens. The church, on the other hand, is the community's chief--and often *only*--source of entertainment. It is the center of young people's social lives and even the object of inter-city rivalry and competition.

April 18, 1854   Grafton, New York

Dear Sister Abigail

I have just recieved your letter of the 8th and was very glad to hear from you agin. I began to think you was not going to write to me anymore and was gladly disappointed.

*We had an exhibition what **(that)** was an exhibition! I had a good many offices to perform. We had to go one day and trim the church. We had a wreath of evergreens go around the church looped up over each window with a bouquet of flowers and a bunch at each corner of the gallery. The stage was built out from the pulpit to the first slip **(pew)** and curtains from the windows clear across*

then we had trees   balsam trees that almost touched the ceiling   the prettiest trees you ever saw just alike slim and pretty   these stood at the corners of the slip on each side   the trees were hung full of birds lemons candies and so forth and then from each tree was another wreath of evergreens hung full of sugar hearts, white and red which looked very pretty in the evening   under that was a large vase of flowers it was the prettiest you ever saw

i tell you it was splendid   every one that came in was led to exclaim how beautifully they have got the church decorated

*You may ask what was our object   there was a select school **(religious training school)** kept at the same time in great big Petersburg you see they were going to have an exhibition the same day as our   then they heard when ours was and altered their time untill after ours and then they said they would beat Grafton or they would die on the spot--great pity they didnt!*

but we heard of it and thought if they will beat Grafton they will have to work some   so we started an evening school to meet at the church every day at 5 o clock to practice our performances

then the day came   the curtain drawed and there was Mr Shirley at the pulpit and on each side four little girls he told the subject of their piece

52

and then they walked forward and told their piece and were no more frightened than I am setting here   then the curtain drawed again and you would have thought the church was coming down there was such a stamping and clapping

then other children went on and spoke their pieces and it seemed they stepped so light they didnt hardly touch the floor   then there was a book with compositions and four girls read it   then Elen Burdick and I told pieces that we had written ourselves, and when we were half way through it I had a song to sing   Pa and Franklin would not hardly believe I wrote it   Franklin thought so much about it he went and asked Mr Shirley if he helped me write it

the church was full so that not every one had seats   then came in the Petersburg with their whole force and two big wagon loads from Berlin and they thought they would do something wonderful but the house was crowded and only half of them could get seats which was too bad for them. they were so amazed that they went home and gave up their exhibition because they thought they had better give it up or come out at the little end of the horn **(the pour spout of a powder horn was an opening about one-eighth inch, "coming out the little end of the horn" was a common saying meaning, "ending up at a disadvantage")**   *so much for Petersburg.*

I am getting tired   all of our folks have gone to bed so I guess I will too so good night   Mary

Mary writes to Abigail again soon. As high-minded as the previous letter was about matters of church, this letter conveys a tale of scandalous behavior on the part of Jo Taylor, a family friend.

It is interesting to note the extent to which the community has become involved in the saving of a marriage. An 1854 community is not merely a place to live, but something to which one belongs. People recognize the family as the primary building-block of society, and feel responsibility for one another's well-being. Read on, and learn of the intriguing shenanigans that could take place 150 years ago.

53

April 20, 1854   Grafton, New York

Dear Abigail

Jo has gone off and left Emily   he went up to Schenectady 4 miles this side of the village and went to staying with the girls   he denied being married and Emily heard of the capers he was cutting up

E B Stevens told her to go up there and see him and find out what he was going to do and if he would not do anything nor go back to keeping house to get a bill **(divorce paper)**

so up she went and took her child and stoped at the tavern where he had been boarding and asked to stay all night   The land lady said she could so she took off her coat and asked if Jo Taylor was there   the land lady said no but he had been there and then asked if she was some way related to Jo   Em said she was his cousin

Well says the land lady I believe I have seen him and that child looks like Jo Taylor and folks say he is married and has got one child. Well says Em so he is and I am his wife   so then the land lady sent for him saying there was some one there to see him and he would not come   so they sent again and told him there was a dance a bout to start and down he come

The women took the child into the kitchen and Em went into the bedroom he went into the barroom and the land lady sent her girl in to tell him there was a child that was left there for him and asked him if he knew whose it was   so they brought the child out of the kitchen and he says Yes by God it is mine and then Em come out and went up and shook hands with him and he didnt know what to say for himself   finally he told Em if she would not say any more about it he would come home with her

and so he did   they got to Congress hall and she went into the sitting room and Jordan Tilly & Eb Stevens & some other Grafton folks were there and by and by Jo come in not knowing they were there.   they gave an introduction of her to Jo and asked if he ever saw her before   and she told the whole story   and the men got to asking Jo if he ever met her before and would he like to marry her and have a child with her and gave

Jo quite a time before they let him and Em get home. (**The men were sarcastically role-playing with Joe in order to teach him a lesson.**) *every body said she done just right*

I must stop for want of room and if you can read this you will do well

Your sister

Mary

This letter from Paul Davidson to Abigail and Francis is significant, for it reveals the date--or at least the week--of their departure for Wisconsin. This move not only wrote the story of the remainder of their lives, but also shaped the destiny of their descendants from that moment right up to the present time.

The letter is typical of the writing formalities of the times. The first and last sentences are particularly form-conscious and bear little resemblance to normal conversation. The fourth paragraph contains two oddities. To refer to one's destination as "the good by land" is unheard of today. And, the last sentence of that paragraph is strangely poetic. It is not a Bible quote, but shows Biblical influence.

The paper is further evidence of frugality. The page is a full 12 inches wide, but is only 8 inches long; and one can see where Paul cut off the remainder of the page to save for future use.

Paul refers to a date as "5 inst," which means the fifth of the month. "Inst" is an abbreviation for *instant*, which was a common and redundant way of saying, "the date on which you sent your letter." This appears in many more letters in this book.

This is the second letter in this volume to give evidence of how long it has taken a letter to reach its destination, and in both instances it has taken ten days for a letter to travel between two points within the state of New York.

May 15, 1854   Grafton, New York

Dear Children.

I take my pen in haste this morning to inform you that we are all as well as usual   we received yours of the 5 inst by which you inform us you were to Start for Wisconsin the middle of the week   hope you will have a prosperous Journey, and realize all your expections in the country of your choice.

Our Spring has come at last and vegetation is fast coming forward and trees leaving out   we went to church yesterday   heard an address on Sabbath Schools from a Mr Fennit of Madison University   had a good Sing after meeting and went out east to the schoolhouse in the after noon

brother C. W. Scriven **(fellow Christian and probably fellow church member)** *is about moving off with his family to Brooklyn or Williamsburg to establish himself in the bason* **(tin washing basins)** *business Mr.Shirley and wife came home with us last night and Staid all night   they will commence house keeping this week*

Think of us when you get to the goodby land and let us know your address and how you get along   and Send down the best of wheat that we who do the hardest of the work may not be obliged to eat the poorest of the victuals **(while not a direct quote from the Bible, Biblical influence is evident)**

I have not yet received any letter from Francis--

Mary has commenced her School. and we ar left almost alone as 'Gusta goes to School----we Sit down to dinner with only Asa and uncle Tom----

But I must conclude my short & hasty epistle by Subscribing myself

Yours respectfully & affectionately   P. K. Davison

Ma. Sends her best respects   Says she wishes you had Staid an other week as you do not start as soon as you anticipated

Three days after Paul Davidson's "goodbye" letter, Abigail and Francis have arrived in Buffalo, New York. There they board a Great Lake's steamship which takes them to Milwaukee, Wisconsin. At Milwaukee they pay their freight bill of $11.18, purchase a team of horses, load their possessions into their wagon, and head west 50 miles into the wilds of the hinterland to settle in the community of Whitewater.

In the 1850s south-eastern Wisconsin is being populated by transplanted New Yorkers. New York place names are springing up all around Whitewater--Palmyra, Troy Center, East Troy, Albany, Walworth, Brooklyn, Geneva, Monroe, Monticello, and New Berlin.

Following is a transcript of the bill of lading, while a copy of the original appears on the next page:

Buffalo May 18, 1854

Shipped by F. W. Smith on board Pro. Forest Queen the following property to be delivered as described in the margin in good order on payment of Freight

F W. Smith	*3 Boxes Furniture*
Milwaukee	*1 Chest*
Care	*1 Stove*
Thos. Williams	*1 Brl* (**barrel**)
	1 double Waggon
	1 Bdl (**bundle**) *Bed Rails*

Total Weight less Waggon	*2055*	
at 35 c per 100		*7.18*
Waggon @		*4 00*
		$11.18

(signature)
Clerk Pro. F. Queen

Buffalo May 18 1854

Shipped by F. W. Smith on board
Pro. Forest Queen the following property
to be delivered as described in
the margin in good order
on payment of Freight

F. M. Smith   3 Boxes Furniture
    Milwaukee   1 Chest
Care   1 Stove
Tho. Williams   1 Brl
                     1 double Waggon
                     1 Bdl Bed Rails
                     Total weight in Waggon 2055
                     at 35 c per 100   7.18
                     Waggon @   400
                                      $11.18
                     F. M. Hall
                     Clerk Pro. F. Queen

The original shipping bill for Francis and Abigail Smith's move to Wisconsin via Great Lake's steamship from Buffalo, New York to Milwaukee.

Here is Mary's first letter to Abigail in Wisconsin. As this book is written in 1999, there exists a nearly unbroken chain of housing developments and suburbs all the way from Whitewater to Milwaukee. How wistful to read of "the splendid seas of prairie flowers" which the pioneers enjoyed there.

May 28, 1854   Grafton, New York

Dear Sister,

It is with great pleasure that I have just perused your letter written in Wisconsin. I am glad to hear that you arrived safe at your Journeys end, and that you are in good health and spirits. all I have to regret is that I am not with you in Wisconsin---instead of being here in this state of Grafton

O it is so delightful to hear how you view the splendid seas of prarie flowers that grow and thrive so beautifully in the state of Wisconsin but it is no use to talk about that for it is not likely I shall go yet, if ever, but I hope I shall sometime

I have been to church to day   heard a very good sermon. the Choir set in the Gallery   had very good Singing   Elen Burdick and Mary Davison herself sung Alto   we sung Earnestly for the last tune and we made the meeting house fairly ring. I like my school very much and instead of feeling lonesome I think it very pleasant.

Mr. Shirley and Lady visited my school last monday   I have a very pleasant school, and I think they learn very fast. I have not seen Franklin since before you went away   he has not been home since we had such a time   and if you want to know what kind of a time it was just ask Francis he can tell you better than I can

I went a fishing last night with Mr. Shirley and lady and I shall not tell you who else and caught a reel lot of fish   how proud I felt   the first one I caught--if you had just seen him kick but he could not get off so he had to give it up

59

But I must stop writing and get ready for school for Joseph is going to carry me over to night

now let me tell the news and then I will draw my letter to a close. Emela has got a B O Y   it was born the 25th of this month   I expect it is almost a man by this time

give my love to all the friends in Wisconsin to William in particular   tell him I want him to write to me   I dont take any pride in my writng, dont let any one see this

from your sister

Mary P. Davison

Paul writes a short letter telling of the weather and church events. Again, the original is on an odd-size page; the unused portion having been torn off as an economy measure.

July 9, 1854   Grafton, New York

Dear children

we received your letter to Mary and I learned to night that she had not written to you since----I was glad to hear from you and hope you will enjoy yourselves first rate in that beautiful country

we are all well as usual   we are having Some verry hot weater   is also verry Dry. hay is coming in tighter than last year or year before---- potatoes and other crops look verry well as yet but cannot endure long without rain

we have a verry interesting Sunday School and are a going to have a sunday School celebration on the 25 of July in the grove above doctor Waites----and in August there is to be a Sunday School Jubilee in Berlin when the Schools are to meet from Rensselar, Columbia & Berkshire counties our mr Shirley proves to be a real worker and draws good assemblies wherever he goes----he teaches a Juvenile Singing School Saturday afternoons, and the children are wide awake learning to sing

I have got my house in Troy about nearly to plaster. the basement of brick & stone is of good height to finish in to a dwelling room and will be but 20 steps below the side walk. the building above is a story and a half with two good lodging rooms above. The house and barn when finished will be worth about 500 dollars

I have been offered 50 dollars advance on the two remaining lots but shall not sell at present

please excuse my not writing sooner   i had supposed 'till I had undressed to go to bed that Mary had answered you letter----hope you will find a pleasant home and that I may live to see you in it----please excuse haste and imperfections and accept our love and good wishes

P.K. & D Davison

Abigail's brother, Franklin (same fellow as Thomas), writes--with an extremely legible and bold handwriting. It is quite an amusing letter, providing great insight into the humor of the time. The KNOW SOMETHING title of a newspaper which he mentions is, of course, a parody on the "Know Nothing" political party of the time.

Everyday folk speech of the era found an extraneous *a* interjected ahead of some verbs. Franklin is a real practitioner of this folksy trait.

July 15, 1854   Grafton, New York

Dear Sister

I take my Seat now to Write you a few lines to let you know how we are a getting along in the Eastern World if this letter reaches you Which i hope it will   if it does you can have the pleasure of reading that I am Enjoying good health now and So is all of our folks

61

i Should be very happy to hear from you and Francis and know how you are a getting along and What you are a doing   i Suppose you are a raising Wheat that the curnells are as large as Shanghais **(a type of a chicken)** *Eggs and great Corn and pumpkins as large as Flour Barrels and Everything nice as you please*

let me know if you had any doins there on the fourth. We did not have any thing in consequence of the Common Council not getting up a Celebration as they Should have done. a new paper just Started called the Know Something   i must just Write a little of it. it reads thus.

"the glorious fourth Was ushered in about 12 o clock on the morning of last week after the manner most approved on Such occasions. the glorious Spirit of universal liberty predominated in the hearts of our citizens and as their nostrils Snuffed in the pure patriotic trojan air a 1776 Spirit Was disseminated through their veins and they arose in their combined might and as With one impulse to celebrate the day.

at one quarter past 5 o'clock am the day Was ushered in by the firing of pop guns and the beating of tin pans according to programme. about one half past 8 the visitors from the country began to pour in and Shortly these visitors to the number of 25 was distributed through our principle Streets and clustered about the Small beer and gingerbread Stands, imparting a gay and enlivening appearance to the city

at 8 minutes 9 seconds and a quarter past 1 o'clock in the forenoon the procession formed at the jail under command of the grand bombastes and amid the cheers of the assembled multitude and the firing of Chinese crackers and torpedoes marched galiantly off in the folowing order

grand bombastes and his brother Jackasses
Troy Fusilier guards, the bare foot infantry
the poor House guard armed With Slices of graham Bread
Troy Suckers under Command of John Prescott
Dutch corpse, Each Soldier bearing a mug of Lager Beer
Committee of arrangement in a Swill cart Surmounted by an American Flag   on which is inscribed the words Trojans Patriotism Triumphant Genuine Grit, never Say die, Surviving Soldiers of the hard cider campaign

Major General Birch leaning on his Staff
Officers of the west troy Canal Navy
Independent Order of Bummers
Order of Curious fellows free and acceptable
Members of the Bar room
Members of the dont care if i do fellows
Shanghai hens riding on mules
rag pickers benevolent association
and a cart drawn by 16 oxen containing the appropriations
*   for fire Works."*

The Know Something is the greatest paper there is out for fun   If you got
to feeling bad about any thing by the time you had read just a few pieces
you would feel quite relieved

the Grafton Sunday School is a going to have a celebration a week from
next Tuesday in the grove behind the grist mill   Elder Baldwin from Troy
is a going to be present and deliver an oration   I Should like to be there
first rate

Write soon and tell Francis to Write as he Said he Would When he Went
a Way and upon my Word i will write soon   Good Night

yours Affectionately

Thos. Franklin Davison

In previous letters we have come to know the writers as straightforward, unassuming, honest people. We've not encountered any people who are scheming, irreverent, or arrogant. Just when we might be tempted to wish for a time-machine to take us back to this more wholesome society, we come face to face with their struggles with mortality.

This letter from Paul Davidson tells of a cholera epidemic. Virtually unknown to our culture, cholera was a disease associated with filth. There was no plumbing.   There were no window screens.   There

were no sanitation ordinances. Horses and all manner of farm animals were present everywhere, even in towns. Flies carried the disease from unsanitary places through open windows to foods. Cholera victims became violently ill with vomiting and diarrhea which caused dehydration. Cases could be so extreme that victims would die the same day they became ill.

The Harrison West mentioned in the letter is Francis Smith's cousin. Francis' full name was Francis West Smith.

Beginning with this letter, the reader will find in this volume many instances of *smart* being used as an expression of physical well-being.

August 6, 1854   Grafton, New York

Dear Children

After returning from church and spending a short time Singing with Franklin and Mary and the young folks who came home with them   they all went off on a ride Some where and left me alone----So my thoughts turned to the absent ones who   though far away   are yet near and dear to me   and I sat me down to pen a few thoughts & Send them to you by railroad and I hope you will receive them in due time.

Mary has taught her 3 months and will now remain at home with us---- Frank has been up a week but will go back to Troy to morrow----the colera rages in troy to a fearful extent and there has been some cases Some thing like it in Grafton----Harrison West died in Troy a week ago Friday and his child about 1 year old   they were buried the same day. Polly his wife was brought out here to the center and was taken with the colera last Sunday night but Doct. Waite has cured her so she is quite smart

We had an excellent celbration of the Sunday School in the grove a week ago last tuesday----it was Supposed there wer at least 700 people present our food table was 140 feet long and well spread with pies, frosted cake &c. &c. which was well received by the hungry throng----(It was a "pot luck" meal in which everyone brought a serving dish to share.)

64

We had good Singing by the Juvenile choir combined from 8 schools who had been trained by our preacher Mr Shirley--who by the bye we find to be a verry profitable man among us----the day was fine and all passed off agreeably----there is to be a great church gathering in Berlin on the 22nd of August   I think Society will tend upward as there is an unusual attention paid to church, Sunday Schools, and Juvenile Hymn Singing Schools

our season has been verry dry----haying come on early and grass light---- hay is worth 15 dollars a ton in the barn

people about here have almost all got the western fever and want to sell out and go to Wisconsin----but when every body wants to sell who is going to bye

write often and tell us about your fine country-----and believe me

Yours Affectionately P. K. & D Davison

Abigail's brother Franklin writes only two days after Paul's previous letter. He, too, reports the cholera outbreak. His closing line, "I wish I was out there to see the tall corn and everything nice," expresses that he has had quite enough of death all around him.

August 8, 1854   Grafton, New York

Dear Sister

I now take my Seat to Write you a few lines to let you know how we are a getting along here in the East   the first thing to converse about in all cases no matter how driving business is **(no matter how pressing other matters are)** *is the cholera. the cholera has been raging here to an awful rate   the number of cases of cholera for about 12 or 14 days back will average 12 a day and nearly all prove fatal*

Harrison West Died a Week ago last Friday at a quarter before 9 o'clock and he was buried right off just as Soon as his friends could get here

65

Harrisons Child Died also about 15 minutes after he did   they both was buried in one grave   only two days before he was a building his new house

Harrisons Wife went in the country to Palmer Wests and She was taken With the cholery out there but has got Smart again. Nathan Saunders is dead with the cholera.   Henry Stevens was taken very Sick with the cholera morbus but got quite Smart again. i was pretty sick for a few minutes but it went a way

i would like to be out there to night looking at that tall corn and all of those nice things   give my respects to all the folks that went West from Grafton   no more at present   Good Bye

most affectionately yours

T. F. Davison

Francis Smith receives this letter from an old friend who addresses him as "Captain," which harks back to his days in the New York militia in the early 1840s. This fellow, Sylvester Benestet, is even a worse speller than the cast of characters with whom we have by now become acquainted.

The United States' present decimal system of monetary denominations had been in use ever since it was devised by Alexander Hamilton, seventy-some years before this letter was written. Why were Americans conversing in English units of money in 1854?

October 4, 1854   Troy, New York

Capt F W Smith

sir I take the presant opertunity to write a few lines to you and hope these Lines will finde you in good health and well suited with youre farme   I shall start next monday to come out in youre new state if we have our health

66

I saw your father in law yesterday in troy with a load of Potatoes   Some he got 7 shillings Per Bushell   they where well as usal and So is the Rest of the people in Jenral

I Shall live in Janesville Wisconsin   I think I Should Like to have you come and see us   My Brother in law is coming with me in the new state he intends to move up on a farm in doge co **(Dodge County in southwestern Wisconsin)**   *he is a going to work it on Shares*

I should like to see you after I git in Janesville and if you has not got possesion of your farme that we might git at some Kind of Bussiness that will pay for the winter

I hope we may have a good time and soon in that new country   this all at present   write to me at Janesville

Sylvester Benestet

Brother Franklin Davidson writes to Abigail. Here is a serious young man in his teens conversing about his need and desire for further education. He then addresses political issues, and his support of a temperance candidate for governor. His reference to something humorous as, "Ain't that a buster," is a folksy expression long extinct in American culture. And always, there is reference to the tenuous nature of life.

November 6, 1854   Troy, New York

Dear Sister

I received your letter this Morning and Was happy to hear that you Was Enjoying good health and Was Well Suited With your new Situation   i am Enjoyinng first rate health at pressent and am happy to Say that my health is better now by fiffty per cent than it was a year ago this time. our folks are all Well i believe

67

my time is up here the first of this month   i dont know Whether i Shall Stay any longer or not   i am not very particular Whether i Stay because if i dont Stay i Shall go home and go to School this Winter   Mr. Shirly is a going to teach a Select School there this Winter and i believe i can learn more this Winter than i ever could before or than i ever Can after this i can See now the need of a good Education and i believe i Could make good use of my time in Study

i Suppose you have good Schools out there   i Should like to be out there and go to School if it was so i could   When i come out there to see you i Want to have my business here all Straightened up So if i Should like to Stay out there i can do So Without having anything here to bring me back

to morrow is Election and there is four candidates for Govenor   Myron H Clark   Green Bronson   Daniel Ullman and Horatio Seymour   i put his name last because i think him the least fit for the office. he is the one that vetoed that Marine law bill last Spring.   he is on the regular Democrat Ticket. Bronson is the Hards candidate   Ullman the Know Nothings candidate and Clark you understand is the Whigs candidate   he is a Temperance man too. he is just the man i hope will be Elected

Clark will put a Stop to this Rum business   i suppose if Mr Adams **(his boss)** *should See this letter he Would discharge me right off at once   i hope he will get his damd old rum barrels kicked out of doors pretty soon ha ha ha   aint that a buster* **(isn't that funny)**

tell Francis that a letter from him would be very acceptable as i would be happy for him to write about things in general   So good bye

from your affectionate Brother

T. F. Davison

PS i forgot until this blessed moment to say i Shall See your place before long if i live and nothing bad happens

**Paul Davidson writes to Francis and Abigail about his great
excitement at seeing the church flourish.   Once again Paul's
communication reveals his sharp mind and extensive vocabulary.
Most surprising in this letter, perhaps, is the relationship of the
activity to the date. They are having a baptism by total immersion in
a river, and the date is November 19--in upstate New York!**

November 19, 1854   Grafton, New York

Dear Children

*having a few moments leisure I imbrace the opportunity to write you a
few lines and in so doing I shall not be detered by any formality but follow
my wandering thoughts as they Shall occur to my mind*

*I wish you were here to day for it has been a marvelous day   there is a
great stir among the people and I say it is marvelous to see our meeting
house crowded to over flowing notwithstanding that the remains of a
Snow Storm still lingers on our hills and our roads suffer with mud   there
is a great revival of religion in Grafton   and the Lord by his Spirit has
given us a convert in nearly all the several neighborhoods*

*some have desired baptism at mr Shirleys hands----which made it
necessary to call a council and have him ordained which council met last
Wednesday consisting of delegates from the Troy churches Petersburgh,
Berlin, & Stephentown churches*

*the council were harmonious and after the preliminary examination we
had an hours recess when refreshment were prepared in the house for all
who wished to partake. and while the dishes were being removed the bell
rang for Service which Startled Some of our visiting brethren into the
interrogatory--"what! have they got a bell in Grafton?"*

*The Services were verry impressive and as follows   Sermon by Elder
Baldwin of Troy ordaining prayer by Elder Sweet of Stephentown charge
by Elder Warren of Troy right hand of fellowship by Elder Rogers and
proclaiming by Elder Sweet*

69

I had been to Troy the week before and supposing of course that it would devolve on me to prepare the place for baptism I went to work and fixed up the old place down by the sawmill   then I learned that they had got ahead of me and fixed a place at Maxsons dam below the bridge which was very convenient being cleaned out at the bottom and provided with steps

the people came together from all parts of the town and filled the house to overflowing   nearly all went to the water which was intirely surrounded, and as many waggons as could get along in the road all filled with anxious Spectators   may the baptised be like the first sheaf which was anciently presented to the Priest which may be followed by a splendid harvest

I must hasten as it begins to be dark----But I like to forget **(I'm afraid I'll forget)** *to tell you how quick I came to be with you this morning* **(metaphorically speaking)**   *while I was leading the singing with Mary at my right hand and Franklin at my left with Augusta also Standing three or four places removed from me, we come to the beautiful lines "Though Sundered far, by faith we meet Around one common mercy Seat----" Quicker than if conveyed on the Wings of Electricity my mind caught a glymps of my loved Abigail and could almost hear her voice mingling with ours as they ascended in accents of praise to our great redeemer*

with much love

Yours

P. K. Davison

Here Abigail receives a letter from her sister, Mary. The letter is written on the back of the previous letter, written by their father. The letter reveals the innocence of the times. These people are not into role-playing. Their statements are straight-forward and unassuming.

November 19, 1854   Grafton, New York

Sister Abigail

I will write a few lines in Pa's letter to let you know that I have not forgotten you. Pa has told you about all the news so I will tell you what I can think of and call it a letter.

Pa told you there was baptizing here but did not tell you who were baptized so I will tell you here Mrs. Sarah Littlefield Charlotte Phillips Caroline Saunders Hellen Bassett and Sophie Wells

William Parks and family with Fanny start for Illinois to day and now I will tell you that I have got me a new Bonnet and Cloake a new Breast pin worth $4 and a half a new dress and so forth   I have got just the prettiest Bonnett there is in town   it is the color of Ashes of roses made of ribbon with a bow on the back and a blue wreath with strings   so you may judge for yourself whither it is pretty or not

and my Cloake is the same color but I cannot tell you how it is made so I will not attempt to   my dress is plaid and pretty to   my gloves are a darke brown   I tell you all these particulars because I expect you will want to know

now I wish I could be in Wisconsin awhile   I think we would have a fine time   but I must close by sending love to all and there is something else I wanted to tell you but I cannot think what it is so if I think of it I will tell you next time

Franklin says tell you he has not time to write   Asa says tell Abigail I am Churning but shall not be long for the butter has most come and now I tell you I want you to write to me my very important self, and that pretty quicke to--if you please   good bye

from your sister Mary

This letter is from Rachel Burdick, Francis Smith's sister. The salutation refers to sister-in-law, Abigail, as "Sister." The letter's penmanship is beautiful, spelling and grammar are terrible, and content is very revealing of life's details. The letter refers to their brother, John. The reader will recall John. He is the fellow in earlier letters who was leaving his "dam drunken wife," and whose son Daniel was "not such a boy as you'd want and destined to be more dummy than prophet." And, imagine being so cold that writing is difficult!

November 25, 1854   Grafton, New York

Dear Brother and Sister

I now set down to write a few lines to you to inform you that we ar well at present and hope this may find you the same   I was glad to receive a letter from you which I had given up of ever geting it had ben so long   but beter late then never   I hope my brothers and Sisters will not forget me if they are so far to the west

*I have thought of you menny a time since you left here and thought you had forgoten me   I see your mother Davison to **(at)** church and I learnt from her a little a bout you   I hope you never will neglect writing so long a gane **(again)***

John Smith is in Calaforny   he wrote to Nathan and wrote he was well and was getting five dollars a day and was paing ten dollars a weeak for board   Mary his wife and too children Daniel and the baby was here in blackberry time and was here a weeak and a half   she dried some blackberrys and took a bucket full home with her without drying. John put Daniel in the factry before he went a way   Daniel does not like to work in the factry   he likes to live in the country   I wish he suited you and could live with you

You Spoke of Daniel   he would be as glad to come and live with you as you would be to have him   I do not know but he may come some time yet I live in hopes of seeing beter times yet   it is no difrent now then it was when you was hear and i do not think it ever will be betr

72

you did not write eny thing about grandmother   She is not vary Smart **(well)** *when Mary red yor letter granny seys Thare they hant* **(further contraction of *haven't*)** *menchend my name   She thought she was slited*

this you can not read for my fingers is so cold i can hardly hold a pen

good by give my respects to all the folks after receiving a good share yourselves

Rachel Burdick

This letter was written on the back of the previous letter by Mary Ett, Rachel Burdick's daughter. Mary Ett's penmanship, spelling, and grammar are markedly better than her mother's (though punctuation is an undiscovered art with her); revealing that the children of the 1850's were receiving significantly more schooling than had their parents.

December 3, 1854   Grafton, New York

Dear affectionate Aunt

I now sit down to answer your letter   we were very glad to hear from you I had almost given up your ever writing to us   We are well at present and hope these few lines will find you the same

old Grafton looks just as it did when you left only it begins to look like winter now   it snows to day so I did not go to church   it snows fast enough now to have sleighing if it lasts long

our select school commenced last monday   Daniel & I are going   I like the school very well so far   Asa and Augusta comes   there is twenty five scholars now and I believe there is more coming

I am glad you like the place out there so you will be contented   I wish our folks would come out there too but I dont expect they will ever leave Grafton   it is such a beautiful country here   but as for me I could afford to do without some of its delicious fruit and all these nice things for the sake of coming out there

I would like to come out there next fall and spend the winter but I don't know as there will be much danger of my coming   it is so far to come alone

and your walnuts   I wish I had some of them for I like them firstrate   just come over some evening and fetch along a bag full and we will have a good cracking   and that would not be all   we would eat a few

tell Uncle Frank to just send us a specimen of his hand writing   give my best respects to him after receiving a good share yourself   good by

from your friend   Mary Ett

Francis and Abigail moved to Wisconsin at about the same time as several families from Grafton. Francis' brother, Daniel, lived near Francis at Whitewater; and their brothers, Israel and Walter, lived at Clarno--a small town south of Monroe, about 60 miles west of Whitewater. All of them lived on farms at the time; the towns are where they received their mail.

In this letter brother Israel writes to Francis, oddly referring to him as "Sir." Israel has business on his mind, and reveals the concerns of a farmer of his time.

January 21, 1855   Clarno, Wisconsin

Dear Sir

I recieved yours **(his letter)** *last evening   was pleased to hear from and learn that you weare* **(were)** *all well   We are all well at preasent and a gineral time of health in this plase.*

74

I have not Sold my pork   I was at Freeport **(Illinois)** *the 14   Could not Sell there to Suit $3.50 is the highest price paid there this week   It is Worth at Monroe $3.38   I have 42 sell 34 first rate   had all the Corn they Could eat for the last 5 months   they will weigh from 400 to 200 about 10 hogs verry fat Can hardly git up.*

I shall not sell for less then $4. I would deliver at Janesville at the Cars **(the train)** *for $4.   Please write immediately on assertaining the Whitewater Market   also the Milwaukee if you can git any reliable information.*

I want to sell a pare of fat oxen after the threshers come   sold the big oxen for $140   I think you done well in purchising the 80 **(acres)** *there at $17.50   you Could not purchis a good one here for that Sum   the Arnold Back* **(80 acres away from the road)** *is sold for $20 the Duncin 80 in the timber is sold for sevn the Wm Arnold 64 is sold for 18 the John Roberts 80 is sold fir 20*

The Wm arnold place is the Chepist and best bargan   it is a first rate little place--good house--it could not be had to day for $30

Write the frait **(freight charges)** *from Janesville to Whitewater per 100 for hogs on the Cars. do you understand*

I must stop Br **(brother--meaning fellow church member)** *Cullip is at the door.*

Israel Smith

This letter is to Francis and Abigail from Francis' brother, Walter. He signs his nickname, "Watey." The letter is poignant for the painful distance which separates the brothers. In point of fact, the distance was only 60 miles; but brothers could live a mere 60 miles apart and simply have no opportunity to get together. With the technology of the times, those 60 miles were a greater obstacle than 600 miles would be today. While Wisconsin was the first state to have

signs identifying roads by number, that practice was 60 years in the future. Roads were dirt and barely distinguishable from farm lanes. The railroad extended to Janesville, about half the distance. Horse travel was too slow to permit a 120-mile round trip in a single day, and farm animals couldn't be left unattended for more than a day. And, there were no telephones.

This letter is significant, too, for it includes a recipe for lard candles.

February 9, 1855   Clarno, Wisconsin

Dear Brother and Sister

It is with pleasur that I once moar find time to seat myself to write a few lines to you   we ar all well at presant   it is a general time of good health in this place   allthough sickness and death is in our land   this is the lot of mankind

Israel was vary sick with the flue   it is awfull it is a dreaded complaint at one time it took three to keep him from fainting   his blood had no circulation   he was without feeling   with good luck and the best of care he got well   he is healthy since

it seams a long time since you left hear   I shold be happy in deede if I cold see you and speeke face to face but that is denyed me by distance and cold weather   I often say how I wish Fransis and Abilgil cold come over on a sunday   it wold be so plesant but it cant be

1 week moar has past away and my litter not finished but will try to compleat it to day

I have no knews to tell of interast only Israel talks of driving pigs to Madderson **(Madison)** *and the store burned with all its contents the loss was 700 dollars*

You asked me for to receit **(for the recipe)** *for lard candles* *tak 10 lb melted lard i lb Salt peter 1 dr* **(dram)** *alum   desolve boath together in brass and boil it till the compisition cakes in the botum of the kettle   be carfull not Scorch the lard   when it is done, drean* **(drain)** *the lard from the kettle   take the sedement out of the kettle and put the lard back and then mold you candles   the less you heat it the whiter you candles will be*

Abigil I wish you wold bast **(would baste)** *for me half a block of Lucy Quilt* **(a quilt pattern)**   *O how I wish I cold come and git it   if I do not come you must take the will foar the deede* **(understand that I would have come if I could)** *and send the quilt in a letter*

Watey Smith

This letter tells such a tale of human woe, that one would wish it were an "April Fool's" letter. Life and well-being seem to hang by a thread in every sentence of this letter from Walter.

April 1, 1855   Clarno, Wisconsin

Dear Brother and Sister

It is with much difficulty that I seat myself to say a few words to you   in the first place I will confess my rong if any thear be of not answering you kind letter   our time was all spent in geting the girls redy for hous keeping

then Israel killed his pork   the first hog they killed bit his hand vary bad at that time you know I must had all I cold do to take car of my meat   the next week was quartly meeting **(quarterly meeting of church supervisors)** *which I know you kind heart will take for an apoligy*

Israel taked **(talked)** *of visiting you but his hand was to bad fir him to be from home   the next week he took a severe cold and he was confined almost to the house from that time till the last of March   he was able to bundle himself up and go out to the door but was not able to do the first hands turn of chors*

77

then Marilla went to school and how i mist her   on Monday following Harvy was taken vary sick   we did not think he cold live but God does all things well   it is now eight weeks this morning

I took sevear cold on my lungs and in my head   the cold in my head was very painful but nothing like the one on my lungs   it is now four week and most of the days I cant Set up   I am vary feble and have tired my self out writing this   some times I think I will never get well

I expect every Mail to hear that Mother is dead

anser this and I will try to live to anser yours

Watey Smith

Paul Davidson writes and tells something of his political life. The opening paragraph is quite an eloquent example of the flowery beginnings which were in vogue in letter-writing at the time.

April 24, 1855   Grafton, New York

Dear Children

in haste I write a few lines to bring to mind my tender regard for your well fare and hope You with us may be enjoying the blessings of health--which is above all things so essential to our enjoyment in this life

we have had a verry pleasent Sunday to day   had two meetings and tolerable good singing and good presenting----Mr Benj. Hayner and Miss Mercy Allen were married last evening and attended church to day

We had a verry Stormy day for town meeting   I was however retained Supervisor by 16 majority over Eliphalet Steward my opposing candidate notwithstanding all the efforts of himself--Scriven, Wells and Parks Backed up by what influence they could get from Troy----and the absence of yourself *while they were doing their best whith whiskey, Shugar and <u>money</u> to bring up the <u>fag end of the party</u>,* **(fag meant *tired* or *weak*. The *fag end* of the party would be those who are easily swayed.)** *the better part of the Democrats were erasing their bully candidate whose watchword was that all H* **(good Christians didn't say "hell" then)** *could not prevail against him, and pasting Paul K Davison on the ballot* **(he was a write-in candidate)**

Affectionately yours P. K. Davison

Mary Davidson writes a brief note on the back of her father's letter. There are separate school terms for the summer and the modern conventional school year, and she is apparently planning to teach one in New York and one in Wisconsin.

April 24, 1855   Grafton, New York

Dear brother and sister.

it is with pleasure I embrace this opportunity of writing to you. we are all in good health. we have had two sermons to day   elder Rogers preached this forenoon and elder Joshua Lewis this afternoon.

you wrote that the fall term commenced in August----but did not say what time **(date)** *I want you to write what time for I cannot possibly get there before the first of September because I have engaged to teach School four months and commence one week from tomorrow at the red school house.*

I am not going to write much mor as it is getting quite dark

from your sister, Mary J. Davison

Brother Franklin Davidson writes to Abigail about religion. He has always been involved with the church (Paul Davidson is his father, after all), but has overtly taken his faith to a new level of seriousness.

April 28, 1855   New York City, New York

Dear Sister

I received your letter this morning   Oh I was happy to hear from you I am just going to write you a Short Epistle as I am in a great hurry

You was Speaking about the goodness of God   I can rejoice with you to day   Dear Sister oh I have often been led to ask myself why was it that God has kept me along in my Sins and as great a Sinner as I have been I feell that it was in answer to prayers   yes many prayers has been offered up in my behalf from parents and Sisters and now I feel that he has Answered these prayers for me

Oh Dear Sister remember us in your petition to the Lord and we will do the Same   Mary is getting well very fast   that has been one of my prayers and now you Can see what it has amounted to.   at the time I experienced religion we did not expect her to live   oh want **(wasn't)** *she happy when She heard the glad tidings   oh--say she--I can die happy now but through the goodness of God she will be spared to us awhile longer*

goodbye

Write Soon

T F Davison

Sister Mary writes once again to Abigail about school, health, and small talk. In her last letter she had planned to go to Wisconsin. In this letter she states she cannot. Life is uncertain, and there are so many unforseen variables which can affect one's destiny.

June 13, 1855   Grafton, New York

Dear sister

I again seat my-self to write to you. I am at home to-day. I came home last Saturday afternoon intending to go back Sunday. but it rained Sunday and I caught a severe cold and have not been able to go back yet. Eleanor Burdick staid with me all night Sunday night and at about 3 O clock she got up and called mother to see me die and I could not raise head nor hand in all that next day. to-day I am quite smart

I like school firstrate but this term closes 2 weeks from to day and we are going to have a public examination and so you can see why I am in a hurry. I feell as if I was loosing time. I am staying to teach the Next term which commences the 2 Wednesday in September   So I shall be home through all the cholera season--although it is very thick here already   I see a funeral procession nearly every time I go to or from school--but the most are Irish.

I wish I could be out there this summer but there is no use talking of that any more   in about one year you may look out for the engine when the bell rings for I should not wonder if you should see me coming

I think yours is a very pretty country   Mother is as good as pie and send her respects

I want you to write as soon as you receive this without fail   so good bye

Mary

In this letter we hear from Marilla Smith for the first time. She is the daughter of Walter ("Watey") Smith, Francis Smith's brother. Marilla is a young woman--probably no older than 20--who still lives with her parents and teaches in a one-room country school. Her letter begins with a poem written about the death of one of her students. Youngsters of her time contended with heavier matters than the next trip to the shopping mall.

Marilla apparently has benefited from more education than anyone whose letters we have yet reviewed. Her spelling, capitalization, and punctuation are almost up to twentieth century standards. She employs a long-extinct expression, referring to an unattractive male as "a crow of a man."

And finally, notice the date--July 4. In a real shocking reversal of today's work ethic, she states that since she is sick she had better do a day's work rather than try to go to the holiday celebration. Apparently she has decision-making authority in such matters and is holding classes.

July 4, 1855   Clarno, Wisconsin

Loved Friend & Aunt

As I now sit alone in my school room my mind has been roving far from here and rests upon one that was near and dear to me, so I thought I would try and let her know that she still has a place in my affections, and always will be remembered.

> *"Silly Dale*
>
> *'Twas a calm clear night*
> *   and pale beams of the moon's light*
> *   Shone soft on hill and dale*
>
> *And friends mute with grief*
> *   stood around the death bed*
> *   of my poor lost Silly Dale*
>
> *O Silly, dear Silly, sweet Silly Dale*
> *   Now the wild rose blossoms*
> *   on the little green grave*
>
> *Of my poor lost Silly Dale"*

I am much better than I was, but far from well. I am obliged to board at Mr. Adams as that is the nearest place and I can not walk as far as home. I do sewing for Mrs. Adams but I fear I do not do as much as I ought. She says I do to much but I know better. Ma has been quite sick.

To day is the birth day of our independence but as I am not very well I thought I had better teach school than to attend the Celebration. I hear the rest of our folks are up to Monroe. I hope they will have a pleasant time. I think I feel as patriotic as any of them and feel as thankful for the privileges we enjoy and for the prosperity of our beloved Country. May the blessings of God rest upon this favored spot in my prayers.

July 6th I have seated myself again to try and finish this imperfect epistle. Lucy Ann Arnold is married. She has got a Crow for a man **(an unattractive man)**. *success attend them I say.*

Dear aunt I hope you think enough of me to answer this as soon as you can make it convenient although this does not deserve any answer, but I know your goodness and shall expect you to forgive me.

I mean to go and see you as soon as I can and think that may be this fall. Kiss uncle Frank for me. He kisses you enough without me telling him to do so.

I must call school **(ring the rooftop bell)** *so good bye till the next time*

Marilla R. Smith

Abigail's brother Franklin writes a short letter on a Sunday morning. The letter is stiff and formal--the influence of his newfound religion, his mood, or advancing maturity? An archaic expression which bears explanation: "going into a store" means "being employed in a store."

The envelope for this letter measures a mere two by four inches, is beautifully embossed, and sealed with hot red wax.

Dear Sister

It is With great pleasure that I Seat my Self this morning to converse a little While by the Way of pen and paper With a dear Sister and friend that has been absent So long.

I am enjoying very good health to gather (**together**) *with the rest of the family and hope these few lines Will find you enjoying the Same blessing. I wish I was out to Whitewater to go to church with you this morning but I dont know as that will be So this fall   as I am about for going into a Store again. But I think of visiting you before a great While.*

I Should think that your village of Whitewater must be quite a place according to the description and advertisements given in the White Water paper.

It is a getting to be nearly Sabboth School time and I must draw these few lines to a close   you must Excuse me for not Writing more this time/although I think it matches yours very well

give my respects to Francis and tell him that i want him to Write to me. With these remarks allow me to bid you good morning

From your Brother

T F Davison

Here Rachel Burdick writes to her brother, Francis, from Grafton. She mentions their aunt, Hannah Smith--a person not to be confused with Francis' future wife, Hannah. Rachel mentions a man named, "Raiment." This is a frequent term in the King James Bible, meaning "clothing." Her literacy perhaps does not extend very far beyond the Bible, and she probably erroneously used this spelling for the name "Raymond." "Jaw" usually meant to talk, but here Rachel uses it to mean "scold."

September 16, 1855   Grafton, New York

Dear brother and sister

I now seat myself to answer your kind letter that I received a few days ago I was verry glad to hear from you and hear that you was well but was very sorry to hear that Minerva was so sick and hope she will recover   I have been to see aunt Hannah Smith   she was well . .   I suppose Israel has been there and made you a visit   he has been here He and his wife   I was very happy to see them and should like to had them make a longer visit   He talks as though he lived in a pretty nice place and I expect he does and I should like to go and see it but we have farmed it some in Grafton this year as well as you have out there   We had a great deal more hay this year than we did last   We raised a piece **(field)***of wheat a very nice peice   We think there will be enough to last a year and we have got a nice piece of corn too and buckwheat*

Jeremiah carried **(in a horse-drawn wagon)** *a load of lambs and wool to Troy the other day and got $53 for it so I guess we shall live through the winter if nothing happens to us   We dont expect to make any thing more than a living here and I dont know as we need any more*

I should like to take a peep into you cottage to day and see how you looked and enjoyed yourself   I suppose you have heard that Raiment Durkee has been very sick but he is getting better now   He is so he can get into a wagon and ride up to Leonard Scriven's but he may not get well after all   It makes his wife mad if any one says any thing about his not getting well   She acts very foolish about it   She has got all of her neighbours mad at her   She jaws **(scolds)** *most every one that goes to see him*

Mary's school is out next Tuesday and I am very glad of it so she can help me   Daniel grows like a weed   he says something about going to live with uncle Frank very often   he wishes he was there now

dont wait so long as you did to write before   I thought you never meant to write again   I will close my letter by saying good by

From your sister Rachel

Here is another letter to Abigail from Marilla Smith, written in her immaculate but tiny handwriting. Marilla's previous letter was sensitive and deep. This one is more trivial. Her previous letter was an excellent piece of writing, technically; in this letter she lapses into practices more typical of her contemporaries.

She mentions again that Lucy Arnold has married a "crow" of a man. She uses the term *spliced* to mean *married*. And, she uses a then-common contraction of *allow* which she spells *'low*. The phrase "I 'low" means something along the lines of "I bet" or "I guess."

December 9, 1855   Clarno, Wisconsin

Dear Aunt

You can not imagine how surprised I was when I received that letter from you for I had long ago concluded that you did not mean to write to me but am glad that I was mistaken. I was glad you were all well. This leaves us all in usual health

Almon is teaching school this winter 10 miles from home   he is to have 50 dollars for three months   He was home yesterday   says he likes the business well. I have partly engaged a school for myself but think I shall give it up   it is to far from home to suit me   It is 6 miles west of Monroe **(making it about 12 miles from home)**

Wm Arnold was down here this fall   Said Lucy Ann was married to a real crow **(ugly man).**   *Mary Dickson Starr has got a daughter   we have singing schools at our school house* **(singing schools were church-related and usually taught by the local minister. And, nobody would raise the specter of "separation of church and state.").**   *I told ma when she was writing to you to tell you that if you did not write soon you would never get another letter from M. R. S.   No that did not mean i was going to get spliced* **(married)**. *I 'low I shall not bid adieu to "sweet single" life in one year to come but reckon I shall come and see you when I do*

Oh dear Aunt how I wish I could see you sometime. Bu La me it's no use fretting   When the right time come I shall see you   I hope you will not leave off writing to me again for fear you will weary my patience for it is not lengthy letters I complain of but short ones

Kiss yourself for me or if that is to hard just change places with Uncle Frank and kiss him for me   It is getting dark and I must close

Yours truly

Marilla R. Smith

This is the only letter which was saved from 1856, the year that Brodhead, Wisconsin was founded.   In the letter Paul Davidson writes to Abigail and Francis. Abigail was named for her mother, and it is she about whom Paul writes.

Paul Davidson has seen his wife and three of his children die, yet every comment he makes regarding these events is positive. He sets a sterling example of the fact that our *attitudes* are not externally thrust upon us, but something we choose for ourselves.

September 29, 1856   Troy, New York

Dear Children

having just returned from our Sacramental Service and being rather lonely I thought I would drop in and converse a few moments with you and being a thousand miles off   I have to take this silent way of communicating with pen and paper

today i tell of my reflections associated with my visit to the old grave yard----after reading the lines on the stone at the head of my little Algina- and my Sweet little Lois I next parted away the brakes **(weeds)** *which partly covered the epitaff of the Sprightly Seraphim   my mind returned to the Scenes of her Sudden Sickness and death and the candid profession of the hope She had in the pardoning mercy of him who said "Suffer the little children to come unto me and forbid them not, for of such is the Kingdom of Heaven." She said she thought he forgave her sins about the time that Abigail and Sally were baptized.*

I cannot doubt that She is indeed an angel leading her infant sisters through those blissful fields of Paradise and tuning their sweet voices in praise to Him who thus early in life took them from this world of care & sorrow to that of eternal peace and joy

then came the tall white marble crowned with that sweet name Abigail--- filling my verry Soul with emotion as it called up in my mind the form and many virtues of my loved one who was the companion of my brightest days----I say many virtues for I can bear testimony that I never was acquainted with one who combined more of the qualities that make up the character that merits the confidence and esteem of all than those which were hapily blended in her

but I will not stop to communicate as you can recollect and I hope will imitate her examplary Christian deportment and Stn'dt **(standard)** *regard for truth and veracity. I remmember in conversation with her before her death of my future prospect I remarked if it were not on the childrens' account I would be willing to go too. She Said She wanted me to stay and take care of the children which I promised if I was spared to try to do---- and have remmembered the promise and no other connexion I trust ever has or will divirt my course from the accomplishment of that object.*

and while her dying members rest with Jesus her dying hand will rejoin with mine in the hope of meeting again in the bright morning of the resurrection.

But I must hasten as it is almost time for church and we have a union Sabbath School meeting to night at the church below the Court house in Second st--

I wish you could visit us and spend a few weeks with us in our new home and tell us all about your fine country but we will wait with patience and if life and health is preserved hope we shall meet sooner or later I mean to see your country when I can conveniently leave home.

please write on the receipt of this----and believe me to be your affectionate father

P K Davison

This letter from Paul Davidson is just to keep Abigail and Francis in Whitewater, Wisconsin up to date on the happenings of the family back in New York. It gives insight into details of daily life--standards and practices of a now totally unfamiliar world. Paul mentions spending time with his team. No, he is not coaching a sport (nobody was in 1857). His team is comprised of two horses and his activity with them is work. The "forwarding office" is a business which delivers freight by horse and wagon--comparable to a trucking company today.

June 29, 1857   Troy, New York

Dear Children

having just returned from Clifton Park I thought I would write a few lines to let you know that we are all well   aunt Mary Stevens is up from New York and says Franklin and Mary are all well and apparently doing well.

I want to see you verry much, and wish I was able to come out but dont know as I can this summer   Hope you can come and see us and all the rest of the folks soon.

We have had a verry wet cold Spring and backward   I have been quite busy making improvements on my place in grafton----have let it all out on Shares and they seem to be doing well. I have a good young team with which I am busied the most of the time

we keep 4 cows here this summer and sell about 8 dollars worth of milk a week which helps us considerable   Asa is engaged in a forwarding office at 12 and a half dollars per month   Augusta is out to uncle Exellars in Napan on a visit----widow Baxter is married to Dea— Waterbury **(Deacon Waterbury)** *and gone to Nassau to live   They have sold the farm to R. P. West who has moved into the house----But as I am getting Sleepy hope you will excuse me and accept this hasty and imperfect Scrawl from Your affectionate father*

P. K. Davison

In this letter Abigail is addressed by her sister, Mary. In a society where business and physical labor are taboo on the Sabbath--and secular entertainments are practically never available *any* day of the week--an all-day church event is eagerly anticipated.

July 24, 1857   Grafton, New York

Dear sister

I am again seated at the table with pen in hand in order to write to you. You must excuse me for not writing before for it has been a very busy time with me as well as all the rest. I am at home now and shall be untill Wednesday on account of our Sabboth School celebration which comes off to-morrow. We hope to have a very pleasant time. I will tell you the arrangements

We meet to-morrow morning at the Church at 9, O, Clock A. M. and form into rank and march by fours dressed in white with Blue Felt ribons for Teachers and a Bow on the shoulder and Hair ribon for the Scholars of the same color   Then they are to march to the Grove where the Camp-meeting was held.

after the morning addresses we are going to have dinner   we are agoing to have the table set back by where the Spring is in the Grove. we will have nine speakers some in the morning and some after dinner and with music from the choir after each   We expect a number of Ministers, one from Berlin, one from Hosick falls one from Sandlake one from Pestenkill one from Troy and so forth

love to all--write soon to your affectionate sister

Mary Davison

P. S. please excuse all mistakes for Asa is over my shoulder reading and making so much noise that I can hardly tell what I am writing

Pa sends love

Franklin Davidson writes a brief "just-to-keep-in-touch" letter. Yet, the letter is quite newsy. It announces his upcoming marriage-- though don't look for the word *marriage* or any conventional synonym. He calls it "hitch traces," an equestrian term.

Further, one can almost hear his New York dialect of the time as he spells things phonetically--*Varmount* for *Vermont*, and *darter* for *daughter*. This is nothing like a New York dialect of today, and illustrates that the language is in a continual state of evolution.

Franklin employs a humorous euphemism--referring to a man's face as his "tobacco soaker." For the first time he refers to himself as Frank, possibly defining a new identity to go with his mature marital status.

November 26, 1857   New York city, New York

Dear Sister

It is a long time Since I have Written to you or even heard from you. Please Excuse my negligence in Writing   though I dont know Which Wrote last   you or me. I am in New York now as you will See in a wholesale & retail feed and Grocery Establishment   this card will tell you Who I am with and where I can be found.

I have not heard from our folks in Troy in about 2 weeks So I do not know what they are up too. I am going up to Troy in about 3 week and also to Varmount as I intend to hitch traces **(get married)** *with Deacon Brown's darter* **(daughter)** *of middletown varmount about Christmas day   I blieve She and Mary have Set the time   I have had nothing to do With it. I Should like to have you and Francis come down firstrate if you can make it convenient and we will have as Merry Christmas as you ever heard about in vermount*

Please Write Soon and let me know how you are prospering. tell Francis I Should like to See his tobacco Soaker **(face)** *once more. please Excuse me for not writing more this time as my dinner hour is about up*

From Your Brother   Frank

91

Abigail is addressed here as "much loved aunt," by Marilla, even though Francis is her blood relative. The two have struck up a great relationship. The last line makes a self-deprecating reference to the quality of the letter. The penmanship is beautiful, and the stationery is embossed and even gilt-edged.

This letter wishes Abigail a peaceful and joyful new year; and happily, none of the players in our story can see into the future and know that 1858 will be the last full year that Abigail lives.

December 31, 1857   Clarno, Wisconsin

My much loved Aunt,

I have concluded to write to you just once more and will then give up writing until you see fit to answer me,

I was very glad to see uncle Francis, but I told him that I was not half as glad as I should have been if you had come too.

I do not teach school this winter but have been away from home ever since last Aug. I was sewing. I came home two weeks ago and shall stay all winter. I did think that I should have come out to Whitewater but certain circumstances have occurred to prevent. I would be very glad to see you and have a good long visit with you. I know that if you knew all that I have pressed through since I saw you you would surely pity me, but I guess I shall live through it all for I now bid all dull care begone.

This is the last day of the year and I wish Aunt Abagail a very happy New-Year and I hope that peace, joy, and plenty will attend you not only the coming but all the years of your life. Uncle Frank says he is lonesome here without you and thinks he will never go off from home to stay so long again without you. I am 'right glad' to hear him say so for I think perhaps you will come out ones in a while too.

O! I have quite a compliment for you dear Aunt. A certain man by the name of F. W. Smith told me to day that he thought that you are a real

92

good sort of a woman and he went so far as to tell me that he believed he thought more of you than I do. Now, dont you think that was calling my affections into question?

Do you remember "Neversee" **(her nickname for a boyfriend who seldom came to see her)** *he is now in Kansas he is still single and waiting for my humble self, so he says; dont you think he is quite devoted.*

I trust you will excuse me for thus intruding this miserable piece of writing upon you

So now good bye, Faithfuly yours Marilla Smith

Our visit to the year 1858 begins with a letter to Abigail from brother Franklin. In his impeccable handwriting he briefly relates matters of--what else--work and health!

February 14, 1858 New York City, New York

My Dear Sister

It is along time Since I have written to yu or any one else but I have commenced writing this morning and I am bound to put her through you will please excuse me for not writing to you Sooner and I presume you will when you learn that my time is all taken up in the store day and night you may Say Saturday nights I am in the Store untill 12 & one o clock at night and I feel to lazy to write you

I understand that Frances has let out his Farm and is coming east this fall I am sure I shall be very happy to see you Augusta will visit here She is to stay in N York sometime I believe She is staying with mary now She has not visited us but one afternoon in Consequence of the Small Pox there has been 3 or 4 cases in the Same house with us but they all got well it has been very plenty in this vicinity this winter

we are all enjoying very good health at present and I hope this little Epistle will find you and yours Enjoying the Same blessing give my respects to Francis and tell him to write when you do I want to hear from him.

Please to answer this at your earliest Convenience and oblige your

Brother

T F Davison

On the back of Franklin's letter, his new bride writes. With distances great, travel nearly impossible, and communication only via letters Frank's new bride and Abigail have never met. This letter is an introduction. What's the new bride's name? Mary! Yes, there are now two people named Mary Davidson--Mary *J.* Davidson, in point of fact--but fret not, the "new" Mary has the presence of mind to use her middle name to avoid confusion in the family, and henceforth calls herself "Jane."

If handwriting analysis has any validity, this new member of the family is a bright lady possessing outstanding character. Her penmanship is beautiful, her grammar and spelling inordinately good for the times. Read on, and see how people handled a socially awkward situation which does not happen nearly as often any more.

Kindly regarded Sister

As Frank has been writing, I thought perhaps a few lines from me would be acceptable -- But I can truly Say I hardly know what to write, for it is the first time I ever attempted to address a stranger, and I am Sorry to Say that Such we are to each other at present   I can recall to memory the time when I visited you when you was living in Grafton, but that is a long time ago

I hope at some future time we Shall not be as strangers. I suppose you intend & come to this place this Summer or fall and then we Shall Expect a long visit from yourself and husband

94

As it is now church time I will close, hoping you will not take this long delay for an example but write Soon and remember me as your friend and sister

M J Davison Jane

This letter from Paul Davidson to Abigail and Francis tells of the happenings of Paul's world: the doings of the church, the troubles of a friend's household, the pride in his own family, reference to the "Panic of 1858" (financial depression), and the need to go milk the cows. It's about life.

The letter mentions an I. A. Allen going into partnership in the lumber business. This Ira Allen is the brother of Hannah Allen. None of our characters know it yet, but in a year Abigail will be dead and Hannah Allen will become Francis' wife. A letter 40 years in the future will tell of the death of Ira Allen and the tremendous fortune which he wrought from the lumber trade.

In the gentile verbiage of the times, delicate matters were not stated with any directness. The letter mentions "interesting circumstances" and "her troubles," and the context of both terms leads us to conclude that what is meant is *pregnancy*.

March 16, 1858   Troy, New York

Dear Children

I received a letter from you Some time Since by which I was glad to hear of your good health and prosperity in your far off home -- we have had a warm winter with but little snow, and it is now quite warm and mudy

We hear from a friend who visited New York on the cars **(took the train to New York)** *that all is well with our folks there--it was hinted that Franks wife were in interesting circumstances*

Henry E. is Gone into partnership with I. A. Allen in the lumber trade, John Stevens having sold out to them and is about to take up preaching a young daughter of C. W. Scriven who owns the Grafton house has Sworn her troubles upon Irvin Waite, Doct. Waite youngest son   this is the topic of much talk and party feeling which is aggravated by the fact of their all being members of the church -- I am verry sorry the old Doctor has such troubles in his old age

We begin to hear the factory bells which have been still nearly all winter and there is hopes that business will revive

I still have hope to be able to visit you in your country Some time but dont let that hinder you coming down here. I have some lonely hours on account of my family being So scatered. but have reason to be thankful that they all Seem to be doing well and are engaged in honorable pursuits

I must draw my letter to a close as I have my cows to milk and want to go to meeting this evening -- I remain as ever Your affectionate Father

P. K. Davison

This letter from Paul Davidson is in answer to one which has taken between one and two months to travel from Whitewater, Wisconsin to Troy, New York. On the same paper is a letter from Abigail's step-mother, Deborah, and from her youngest sister, Augusta. The letter from Deborah is in Augusta's handwriting, and Augusta's letter ends with mention of "having to write a few lines for ma," as Deborah cannot write.

April 3, 1859   Troy, New York

Dear children

Your letter written in February was received week before last by which we were glad to hear from you. we are all well as usual and all our folks in New York as far as heard from. we have had a verry mild winter and it bids tolerable fair for a early Spring we have talked some of moving back to Grafton this Srping and hire out **(rent)** *our houses here but dont know as we Shall   I have built another house on the North East corner of my lot which I can rent for 7 dol* **($7)** *per month.*

we have been to church to day and had a verry good meeting. there was one baptized----Elder H. J. S. Scriven is to remain in Grafton this year and preach to the church   Elder Cobb is still living there----Doct. Waite has been quite unwell this winter and has some Discouraging Simptoms. John Tilley has moved to Port Schuyler with his whole family except his oldest Daughter who married Andrew Pickham and lives on the old Pearley Reynolds place   Your cousin Julia Eliza is here on a visit   She has been to Maine & Newhampshire

we have heard Sad news from Illinois about a difficulty that has Sprung up in the Davidson church there and threatens to do much hurt to the cause of the young church on the Prairies   the muss Seems to grow out of a circumstance in which Harvey punished Rowlands son Lee in school.Being all church members it has caused a division and about 1/3 of the members have withdrawn.

I want to see you verry much and will come out if I possibly can but don't set your heart upon it too much and be disappointed if things Should so turn out that I should not come

I promise I will not be so long again in writing   With my ardent prayer and solicitude for your health and wellfare in life, and a joyful meeting with you and our beloved ones in Heaven I subscribe myself

your loving Father

P. K. Davison

Brother Frank Davidson writes to Abigail with a very brief letter which bears bad tidings and expresses profound depression. In Frank's last letter, which was in February, he mentioned neighbors having small pox. Now his new bride is ill with the disease.

April 19, 1858   New York City, New York

Dear Sister

I received your good letter

Jane is very sick and they consider her very dangerous **(very dangerously ill)** *the Doctor says now that there is Some hopes of her recovery   her disease is the Small Pox   the rest of us are well at present and I hope you and yours are all enjoying the Same blessing   my mind is so taken up with other things today that I hardly know what I am about   so I hope you will excuse me to day*

Some other time I will write you more   I want you to pray for me dear Sister that I may not falter   Gods Strength alone can bear me up

these few lines from your unworthy brother

T F Davison

Brother Israel Smith writes to Francis and Abigail from his farm near Monroe, making one of the rare references to Francis as "Captain." He mentions that the rail line from Whitewater is now complete as far as Monroe. And, he talks mostly about what fills his mind--farming.

July 12, 1858   Monroe, Wisconsin

Dear Brother & Sister

After so long a time Sinse I heard from you, I thought I would write a fue lines. We are all Well and it is a gineral time of health in the County. I have not commenced haying and am not done plowing corn   it is very mudy.

I am sorry I did not know in time that you would have worked for me in harvest   I have my help ingaged and paid or a-part paid. and have but little harvesting to do. I pay for hands **(workers)** *in corn 50 cts per day, in haying 75, in grain $1*

98

tell old Burrows I am on hand for a trade of farms. As he nor I can Sell at our prices at the present and it is hard times for money.

you and Abby come see us. write three or 4 days before you come and Say the day you will come and I will be in Monroe with a team to meet you on the cars. you will git in about one half past 6. pm. it is to far for ant abby to walk

Israel Smith

Finally brother Franklin has reason to be in a more upbeat mood and shows some humor in his letter. Some things hinted at in previous letters are, indeed, factual. But why spring the punchlines ahead of time? Read the fun for yourself.

August 9, 1858   New York City, New York

Respected Sister

I received your letter this morning and was happy to hear that you are in the enjoyment of good health &c. We are permitted by the Will of providence to enjoy good health at present

we are expecting in a few days to have an addition to our little family   if that little one should be spared to us   it has no one as yet that it can call first cousin   isnt that to bad. I should think you had better hurry up your cakes   I am afraid you are not much good to the western Country.

We are having very plesant weather here now   We have been having very warm weather   New York is the hottest place in the summer you ever want to see. Asa is here with us now in the Store and makes it go very well with so little experience

I should like to see you and a great many other friends in the West   if I have good luck in business here in a year or two I think I shall travel some in the Western Country.

Jane sends much love to you all

Write Soon and oblige your

unworthy Brother

T F Davison

PS

Tell Francis I should like first rate to see his Tobacco Factory down here in the great metropolis   Tobacco commands a good price here now

Mary Davidson is in New York City, and she writes to Abigail regarding Abigail's last letter. She expresses unrestrained emotion at the news of Abigail's ill health. The letter does not express what the illness is, but in a few months Abigail shall be dead. This is Mary's last letter to her.

A newsy item in this letter is of historical significance. It regards the Crystal Palace, of which Paul Davidson wrote so eloquently. Mary mentions her quilt being destroyed there. Smith's house in Brodhead contained thirty-some quilts, some extraordinary. It is unfortunate that Mary's quilt could not have passed into Francis' and Abigail's hands and thus have been preserved--for think how exquisite must have been this quilt which a conscientious young woman made for display at the world's fair.

The closing paragraph of this letter is hauntingly beautiful and poetic--written from the heart of one who knows these may be her last words to a beloved sister.

October 6, 1858   New York City, New York

Dear Sister Abigail

I received your letter week before last and I need not tell it caused sorrow and disappointment to read it. Pa was here at the time and I indulged in

100

a good cry and he, well you know he never cries, but we all know when he feels bad or is disappointed

We were very sorry to lern of your sickness   afflictions, my dear sister, are to us as the fire to the gold   it leaves us purer and I hope better for having come in contact with them

We had a great excitement here yesterday caused by the burning of the Chrystal Palace which is as flat as can be   I had a bed quilt there which was burned too. I suppose There was nothing saved at all   for within twenty minutes from the time the fire was first discovered   it was all down.   There were a great many thousand dollars worth of things completely destroyed. It is gone, the beautiful Chrystal Palace is gone, and it looks lonely enough around where it once stood.

May God grant that this letter finds you in better health than when you last wrote   So good night, dear sister, and may pleasant dreams attend thy sleeping

Your sister

Mary

Once again Paul Davidson writes on his favorite topic, religion. His letter opens with disappointment at Abigail's cancelled travel plans, and he waxes poetically philosophical on that point.

October 24, 1858   Troy, New York

Dear Daughter

We received your communication last week and was Sorry to hear You had given up with visiting us this fall   we had anticipated much pleasure in having you with us this winter. I suppose we must submit and try to be reconciled to the dispensations of Providence which seems to direct that we cannot meet ere long **(before long)**

Franklin was here yesterday and has gone up to Vermont after his wife and baby who have been up there to her mothers for 3 or 4 weeks.

We had two good instructive Sermons today, the first being on the 8th chapter of Romans   the Spirit teaches us that we are the children of God and as Gods children we are his heirs and joint heirs with our Lord Jesus Christ -- Yet with a strong sense of our unworthyness we are timid and know not what to say to our Heavenly Father   the Lord seeing our imbarrassment kindly assists our infirmity and makes the intercession for us.

O! what wonderous Grace to be enabled to become an heir to all the bliss in the paradise of God and how we are laid under obligation to Give our whole Selves unto God -- i know that Love so amazing, So divine demands my soul, my life, my all. but it is about bed time so I will bid you good night

Yours, in paternal Love

P. K. Davison to his daughter Abigail

PS. the last Sermon was on the temptation of Christ in the wilderness founded on the 4 Chapt of Matthew. We closed with the beautiful hymn by Watts, "with joy we meditate the grave----"

Francis Smith's sister, Rachel Burdick, has a son named, Daniel--not to be confused with their brother's son, Daniel. In this letter Daniel writes to his uncle, Francis. Daniel's handwriting is exquisite. Some of the letter *t*'s are crossed with a tiny feathered arrow penned in a second color of ink. Other words have a gap left in every pen stroke at exactly the same height above the line of writing, and these gaps are filled in with a second color of ink.

Definitive of the era, this teenager is planning with pride to buy a team of horses so that he can do man's work.

The beginning and closing lines of this 1858 letter from Daniel Burdick show the beautiful penmanship of the time. The letter *t* is crossed with an artful arrow. It and other selected pen strokes were done in a second color of ink.

November 19, 1858   New Boston, Illinois

Dear Uncle

I now take my pen in hand to let you know that I am enjoying good health and hopeing that these few lines will find you enjoying the same blessing

I had good luck comeing except at Muscatine my satchel was taken off thare which is 20 miles from New Boston   I went back the next day and got it   We have had pretty good weather here this fall   thar has not many finished corn geather-ing yet here   corn is good here   Wheat Oats & Potatoes are mix   Corn is worth 30 cts

I am agoing to stay here this winter   I have a chance To do choors and go to school   I am agoing to work some land next summer   I want to buy me a team this fall   I can get them a great deal cheaper this fall than next spring

when you send me the 50 Dollars send a check if you can get one   if not send it in 3 or 4 letters   I rather you would not let the post master know anything a bought it

*I wish you would see whither the corn planters like Uncle Daniels are Pattented or not   give my love to all enquireing friends   Write as soon as you receive this   Direct to
New Boston Mercer Co Ill*

From a friend

Daniel L. Burdick

To Francis W Smith

This letter from Paul Davidson provides a great character sketch of a prominent industrialist who has died in Troy. This good capitalist was apparently the antithesis of what one could call a "robber baron." Next, the letter summarizes at length the life of Christ. It

then concludes with a paragraph as prophetic as was the final statement of Mary's last letter.

Not long after this letter is written (early in 1859) Francis and Abigail move to Brodhead, Wisconsin--a small village founded only three years previous, and located along the new railroad line connecting Whitewater with Monroe. Soon after the move, and at the age of 34, Abigail dies.

This is Paul Davidson's last letter to his daughter, Abigail. One can only imagine what this very sensitive man wrote back to Francis when he learned of Abigail's death. Unfortunately, Francis did not save that letter. Abigail must have been the one to save letters, because after her death there is a gap in the collection.

December 12, 1858   Troy, New York

Dear Daughter

having just returned from church I will Spend a few moments in writing to you   we are all well except Franklin's wife who has been verry sick but we are glad to learn is getting better   they have got a precious little daughter who is verry quiet and good

Mary wrote last week and inquired in particular if we had heard from you her health is quite good -- Asa is in New York in a wholesale store. I am engaged this winter building a home on my lot 17 by 34   we talk of living in it ourselves when I get done

business is rather better this winter than last   but has not entirely recovered as it was before -- our Ida Hill has met with a great loss in the death of Benj. Marshall who died week before last   he was the projector **(promoter)** *and owner of nearly all the manufactories on the hill   he has made arrangements by his will that they shall be kept running for a term of years and the profits be given half to the Marshall Infirmary a large institution founded by him for the support of the sick and lunatick and the other half to be divided equally between the trust society Mission & bible societies*

Today my mind reviews the life of our savior -- baptism in Jordan, then his temptation in the wilderness the weding at caanea in Gallillee then the scene at Jacobs well, his visit and rejection at Nazareth then the whip of small cords at the temple and the driving out of the buyers and sellers -- then the momentous fishing Scene at the sea of Gallillee the storms on the lake and then his visit to the accusal city and the events which are the foundation for our religion

i often contemplate those storms on the lake which Seemed to threaten enevitable destruction to the devoted crews and made them cry out for fear and just at the critical moment they thought of their Saviour being on board and found him in the hinder part of the ship where this wearied human nature was taking rest in sleep and upon being wakened by the desiples who were astonished that he could sleep in time of such peril he waked and gently rebuked them for their lack of faith, then arising in all the majesty of God he rebuked the raging wind and maddened waves as a Parent would rebuke a little child, "Peace be still." no wonder that the astonished men cried out "what manner of man is this that even the wind and the sea obey him?"

we must pity the unbelievers who when that last hour shall come and the dark surges of the ocean of eternity Shall be opened in all their dread realities before them shall find too late that all their false hopes are in vain and if Christ is not in their vessel they must sink into endless despair.

But to you Abigail Christ is a present hope in all the troubled Scenes of life and even in the Jordan of death you may so rely on him as to fear no evil. be cheerful and be assured that you are in your fathers prayers without one intervening day. remember your unworthy father in your private devotions and if we cannot meet again in this life by faith shall we meet around one common mercy seat.

much love to you all

P K. Davison

This last letter of the 1850s is from Harvey Smith, Francis' nephew who lives near Clarno, Wisconsin. We close out this chapter with Harvey's interesting tale of the young men from Monroe who have heeded the call of gold in Colorado. It seems that on the rumor of gold strikes, a large number of men have rushed for Colorado--the "Pikes Peak or Bust" gold rush of American legend. Then, on the rumor that the gold rush is over (busted), they turn back toward Wisconsin. The latter rumor, of course, was not true--gold and silver discoveries continued in Colorado with delightful regularity until the dawn of the twentieth century. Harvey Smith will be the leading character in the next chapter.

June 5, 1859   Clarno, Wisconsin

Dear Uncle & Aunt

I seat myself a few moments to write you a line   we are all well as common   father and mother have gone to Monroe to meeting   the minister is the reverend Mr. Bennett   he is a verry smart man   father has rented a pew

I have been dangerously ill and was not expected to live, but I begun to get better about three weeks ago and I have got entirely well and smart I have been ploughing corn and mending fence   night before last was pretty frosty   it killed all the corn and tender plants down to the ground but they will come up again

the Monroe bugle staff has all broken up because the boys have nearly all gone to Pikes Peake   we have heard from them several times while they was on the road   they took thare bugle stuff and things with them

Sylvester Carson the leader of the band wrote home from Council Bluff he says that Pikes Peake died last week which was about the 10th of May and was decently interred   he says we can form no conception of the misery which that d----d humbug **(damned rumor)** *has caused   thare are thousands on the return from the Peake without one cent to buy their victuals with* *there are men at Omaha offering to work at anything to pay the ferry charge accross the river Sylvester and the band gave a concert and took in twenty dollars Sylvesters letter told the following story--*

"a team just drove up the wagon had four men two of the mean were for going to the Peake and the other two for going back they got into a qarrel about it they settle the muss as follows -- they took a saw and cut the waggon in two two of them took the fore part and one horse and the other two the hind part and one horse"

I think Wisconsin the bigest humbuged State and Monroe the bigest humbuged town in the union

Uncle Zeb and Aunt Philena made us a visit since corn planting time give my respect to all of my relation in Whitewater

excuse all mistakes and bad speling for this is the first letter I have written in a long time

Harvey Smith

With the end of Abigail's life, the chapter of her family--the Davidsons--is concluded. One can only wonder how their lives played out over the years, and what became of them and their children's children. Their untold stories are among the millions of vibrant threads woven into the stout fabric that is America.

Finally, there is one of life's lessons to be learned here. Abigail and Francis left New York for Wisconsin in 1854. In the four last years of Abigail's life, she and her beloved family back in New York never saw one another again. Virtually every letter written by every member of the family made a pledge to get together when it would be convenient, or when the crops would be harvested, or when money would be plentiful, or when a better season for travel should arrive . . . when . . . when . . . when . . .until it was too late. This is one fact of life that has not changed with the passing of the centuries--people still say they will take time for one another *when.*

Hannah Maria Allen in a glass plate photo taken in New York city in the 1850s. The price on the back of the photo is marked at "One Shilling."

CHAPTER FIVE

THE CIVIL WAR ERA, 1861-1865

Hannah Moves West

Francis Smith went back to Grafton, New York after losing his wife, Abigail in 1859. There he pursued a relationship with Hannah Allen, and the couple was married in 1860. Francis took his new bride back to Brodhead, Wisconsin.

Brodhead was by now just four years old. It had been created literally overnight as the abuilding railroad split the distance between two villages, prompting the residents of both to meet at the rail line. And so they moved to the central location, dragging their homes and business buildings with oxen.

The scene which greeted Hannah's unaccustomed eyes was vastly different from the visual treats of northern New York. In twentieth-century Wisconsin, ridges which are too steep for farming are covered with trees. Virtually every farm has its acreage of timberland, and woodlots have sprung up everywhere land is not tillable. The southern Wisconsin landscape of the twentieth century is quite similar to that which Hannah left in upstate New York.

But, the landscape of 1860 was still in its natural state. Throughout the millenia which had passed since the last ice age, southern Wisconsin was part of the vast midwestern prairie which burned with sufficient regularity to eliminate all but the sturdiest of oaks, which stood singly and widely spaced on the endless grasslands. Hannah's first view of Brodhead, then, was of a handful of store buildings clustered next to a railroad track and surrounded by a sparse and widely spaced collection of homes. Not a tree was in sight, and Hannah recalled in her old age that she could then see distant hills which the press of civilization long since obliterated from view.

The prairie grasses waved endlessly, interrupted by a tilled field here and there. Streets were sand with manure, sidewalks were sand with a few wooden planks, lawns were sand with weeds. Most homes were surrounded by picket or rail fences to keep wandering livestock out of the yards. Hannah told stories of the difficulty she had in pushing a baby carriage because the wheel rims would sink in the sand. She told, too, how unpleasant a lady's walking could be. While men strode along in high leather footgear, women wore full-length skirts which collected sand burrs.

Along the Sugar River, a mile to the west, the remnants of once-viable tribes of native Americans still plied their route of seasonal migration. On occasion, they would venture into Brodhead to trade their traditionally crafted items for groceries from Francis and Hannah Smith's store. One transaction involved a pair of beadwork-covered moccasins. Another time it was a leather beadwork hunting bag. Finally came the masterpiece--a three-foot-long birchbark canoe which duplicated its full-size prototype in every detail. Francis put it on permanent display in his store.

Hannah, the pretty 22-year-old delved into the hard work which would make her look old before her time; not that Francis was cruel in his choice of a place to live. To the contrary, *this* was considered to be the land of opportunity; and where *wasn't* the common folk's life hard in 1860?

In the decade which followed Hannah's arrival in Brodhead she and Francis lived in two or three rented locations, though their store building remained constant and was destined to be owned by their descendants for generations. During this decade the Smiths had three children. All of them died. Willie died at three months; Minnie at one year. Al lived to be four before falling prey to scarlet fever. His favorite toy was a rocking horse named "Old Kit." Hannah sadly recalled that the little fellow's last words were: "Poor little Al will never ride Old Kit again." The rocking horse remained in the attic, complete with glass eyes, real leather saddle and bridle, and real horse hair mane and tail. An antique dealer paid a thousand dollars for it in 1997.

Wedding picture of Francis and Hannah Smith. It is 1860 and the place is Grafton, New York. Francis is 38 years old and Hannah is 22.

Here are obituaries for the Smith's three children who died. They are reading for the stout of heart, and it is easy to be moved by the lines published for these children who died so long ago.

There is no similarity between obituaries from the nineteenth century and the late twentieth, except that they both mention someone has died. While latter-day obituaries are something like simplified resumes and sound about the same for scoundrel as saint, earlier obituaries spoke from the heart. They talked about the person as a set of qualities and explored what the person's passing might mean to those who remained.

The following are verbatim from the *Brodhead Independent.*

Death of Little Allie Smith

Many of our readers will remember the beautiful little fair-haired, bright-looking, confiding little creature who won all hearts. Little Allie was taken with malignant scarlet fever, and although he lingered between hope and fear, thirty-two days, he then passed from earth, his disease assuming a typhoid form toward the last. Mr. and Mrs. Smith have many warm and sympathizing friends here, in their great affliction.

'Tis the best belov'd and cherished,
    'Tis the beautiful that die--
As the fairest flowers lie perish'd
    When the Storm King passes by.
Like the summer buds they're falling,
    When they hear the master calling.

Such a tiny grave they made him,
    And while many a teardrop fell,
There amidst the gloom they laid him,
    Laid the child they loved so well--
Left him with that silent number,
    Beautiful in death's cold slumber.

113

Think thee, mother, in thy sorrow,
            There's a realm beyond the tide--
Soon may dawn that glorious morrow,
            Bright with bliss so long denied;
But awhile he slumbers only,
            In that grave so dark and lonely.

Many a soul like thine is aching,
            Many a tried and troubled breast,
Many a weary heart is breaking,
            Longing, O! how much for rest--
By the grave, low crush'd and weeping,
            Where some treasured one lies sleeping.

For Minnie Smith

In castle halls, or cottage homes,
Wherever guileless childhood roams,
O, there is nothing half so sweet
As busy tread of little feet.

The sighing breeze, the ocean's roar,
The purling rill, the organ's power,
All stir the soul, but none so deep
As tiny tread of little feet.

At eve, when homeward we repair,
With aching limbs and brow of care,
The voices ring out clear and sweet--
Then comes the rush of little feet.

But when the angel of death has come,
And called the flow'rets from our home,
Oppressive silence reigns complete--
We miss the sound of little feet.

Soft night hath come; all are asleep,
Yes, all but me--I vigil keep;
Hush, hush, my heart and cease to beat;
Was that the step of little feet?

Yes, mother, 'tis the softened tread,
Of her you miss and mourn as dead,
And often in your sweetest sleep,
You'll dream of hearing little feet.

And when this pilgrimage is o'er,
And you approach that blissful shore,
The first to run, your soul to greet,
Will be your darling's little feet.

For Smith's Infant, Willie

They tell me, love, that years will come
　　Between thy memory and my heart;
That time will bring the healing balm,
　　And soothe at least the bitter smart.

But no--I would not have it so;
　　I never--never would forget;
The weary years may come and go,
　　They'll find thy memory dearer yet.

Yet, darling, might the boon be given,
　　I could not call thee back to me,
Away from the pure clime of Heaven,
　　Back to earth's sin and misery.

I would not take thy harp of gold,
　　And give thee, in its place, earth's tears--
Nor for thy crown of joys untold,
　　Give thee a mortal's grief and fears.

But I would have thee sometimes come,
  When shadows thicken 'round my way,
And whisper of that better home
  With thee, in the bright realms of day.

And when this weary, aching heart,
  Feels its slow pulses throbbing low,
And near my feet with joyful start,
  I hear the sullen river's flow,

My angel son, be then there
  To meet me on earth's fading shore,
And guide me to that land so fair,
  Where sorrowing mortals weep no more.

Hannah and Francis kept these things, and surely the sorrow of lost children never entirely left their hearts. Hannah lost three children and then two husbands, and had her full measure of grief--out there on the lonely prairie so far from relatives and her childhood home. This is not to say, however, that Hannah was morose. Quite the contrary, her mood was usually positive. Cheerfully singing hymns was a daily practice as she went about her work. Her favorite: "Oh for a thousand tongues to sing my great Redeemer's praise, the glories of my God and king, the triumph of his grace . . ." And, her sense of humor could even be salty. Once in Hannah's later years, Joyce called out to her: "Grandma, what are you doing so long in the kitchen?" The chuckling old voice replied: "Tryin' to set a rat turd up on the little end!"

Letters From Soldiers

With the Civil War, thousands of lads rallied to the flags of their respective states. Virtually every family was affected by this national tragedy, and the Smiths were no exception. Walter Smith's son, Harvey, was among those to volunteer. Years after the war, Walter's family began to disperse while Francis and Hannah were firmly rooted in Brodhead. Thus Walter gave the collection of Harvey's letters to brother Francis for safe-keeping. He reasoned, too, that the letters should remain in Green County, Wisconsin. And so they did, in the attic.

The letters from Harvey Smith tell with unpolished grammar and honest feeling the attitudes of the common foot soldier. Here was a man of solid character who could understate the privations of a soldier's life and verbalize his country's cause with a simple eloquence.

Similarly came two letters from the soldiery of Wesley Patton. His family lived across the street from the Smith's house, and thought that the Smith's home would be an appreciative repository for the letters.

Harvey discusses firearms in this letter. He says their present guns are "not very true." By *true* he means *accurate*. The gun of which he speaks is probably a firearm which was outdated by the time of the war. At the outset many regiments had older guns which had been converted from flintlocks, and some were inaccurate smoothbores. The model 1861 and 1863 Springfields made in the US arsenal and by a score of private contractors were excellent arms. Even at full production, the North had a shortage of rifles. The Enfield he mentions was a British rifle, and it indeed was considered to be a superior arm. The South was harder pressed for firearms than the North, but both sides turned to Europe to augment the output of their own factories. The Union (North) bought 500,000 Enfields and the Confederacy (South) bought 400,000 of them.

July 7, 1863

Dear Friends

I take the present opportunity of writing you a few lines to let you know where and how I am at present. We are at murfressburou **(Murfreesboro, Tennessee)** *now. We do not expect to stay here very long We are under orders to march All that we are stopping here for is because the Colonel he was arested for driving a sergent out of the Regiment that the Govner sent for the head sergent*

We had a very hard time geting here The roads was so mudy that we could not get along very fast and heavy loaded It rained and when it did not rain it was so warm

on the fourth we had all the new potatoes that we could eat for supper and all the blackberys that we wanted all the time we was on that march The blackberys I never saw the like in my life.

We was drawn up in line of battle once on the road The advance guard saw some negros in the blackbery patch and thought it was the rebels. We are a going to draw new guns here to day They say the ones that we have ways Eleven pounds and they are rather heavy to cary all day and they are not very true eather. We expect to draw the Enfield and they are just what will hit the mark every time

All I ask of you is to write soon No more at present Write Soon

H Smith

In this next letter, Harvey invites his friends at home to come visit him near the war zone. It is a homesick lad's wishful thinking.

September 1, 1863

Dear Friends

I thought that while the opportunity was good I would try and inform you that I am still on the land of the living at the present time and injoying midling good health, but nothing to brag of for I have got the diereas prety bad. We was musterd for pay yesterday. My clothing account is $55.

So far I drawd thre ruber blankets   two woolen blankets   thre pair of pants   two dress coats   one great coat   two pair of shooes   six shirts and three pair of drawrs   one hat and one cap and I suppose that they amount to about 55 dollars

I think that you mite come and see us and while you are a seeing us you will see a great many more things that you will never see at home   go to Chigo and take the Ill sentral **(Illinois Central)** *till you come to St Louis and cincinnati road* **(railroad)** *and then take that road for mitchel and then to new albany then to Louisville then to nashville then to murfresboro and you can get here the fourth day*

we heard that Charleston is ours. and I think that this damn rebelion will be put down in a short time and I hope to god it will for we are all a getting tired of this way of living   if I tell the truth we have saw some prety hard times since we have bin in the service of our country   but hoo cares so we save the union and some of these days we will plant the old stars and stripes where they are now trampled

write soon   no more at present

Harvey Smith

The following letter is a reminder that, as deadly as the Civil War hostilities were, an even greater number of soldiers died from disease.

September 5, 1863

*I thought that while I had nothing to busy myselfe at I would write you a few lines to let you know that I am at the Hospital   they **(there)** was a man died this morning that laid on the bed next to me about breakfast time I am in the third ward   about every one that is very sick and brought in third ward is caried out dead*

they brought a man in here the other day and the next day he was caried out dead   they take about two to the grave yard a day from this Hospital that is the avrige number   and some times more

we have had very prety weather for the last few days back

I have not mutch to write to you but I thought that I would write you one more   if it does not get an answer i will quit   I guess that you have forgot that you had a solger boy in the armey but I have not forgot that I have friends at home   now write and I will forgive you   Direct to Hospital No. one and if you are of a mind put third ward on too

Harvey S

In this letter Harvey reveals that not everyone who served the noble cause was always able to maintain a noble level of conduct.

September 27, 1863

Dear Friends at home

I thought that I would write you a few lines to let you know where I am and how I am   I am at Louisville Kentuckey at Hospital No 4 fifth ward I have bin with a pain under my sholder blaids and a cross the small of my back

the Hospital's here is not worth any thing   A sick man can not hardly get enough to eat   The stewart and them that has a little office they are the one's that get the good things to eat. I understand this very well for I have bin watching there movements for some time   They put one of the stewarts in jail for selling the rations and puting the money in his pocket

we have some nuns in this Hospital to wait on the sickest men   They dress in black and weare a white cap all the time and wear a cross and a string of beeds by there side   they go to there meeting every morning they dress in black from top to bottom and look as solemn as some old deacon

I will bring my letter to a close by asking you to excuse this letter and this poor writing and spelling and ever thing

From you Son

Harvey Smith

Tell ma that when I am a coming home I will bring her something prety.

Now Harvey writes here a more light-hearted letter. Combat is a remote thought at the moment, and he is primarily occupied with thoughts of physical comfort and pleasure.

October 25, 1863

Dear Friends

I thought that I would write you a few lines this morning to inform you that I am well and injoying good health at present   we have a very good time at this Camp   we go where we pleas and do as we pleas   we are a scouting all the time and evry time we go out we fetch in a hog or a beef so that way we have fresh meat all the time   the boys just shot a hog for I heard the gun fire

Sargent Shull went out after some bushwhackers this morning and has not got back yet old Rosey **(General Rosecrans)** *is not doing much now but he is awaiting for an attack*

Ill tell you what I want and that is a pair of Boots and a good pare   I will tell you where to get them at monroe at millers shop   you go and tell Godard that works in Millers shop that you want a pair of Boots the same sise of Sylvester McManas and the same stile and same kind of leather they cost six and a half or seven Dollars   I want them as soon as you can get them maild   start them soon for it is a raining here and this thing of having wet feat I do not beleive in

and while you are doing this send me a pound of fine cut tobaco in one of the Boots   express this through and direct it to follow the regiment

write soon

Harvey Smith

This letter begins with a bit of melancholy. It then shifts to a mentally healthy resignation to the rigors of a soldier's life--and yet, "methinks he protesteth too much."   The letter *ends* with the words, "to Dear Mother."   Such seeming salutations were common closings of the time. Happily, the letter ends on a note of 1860's humor.

November 1, 1863

I thought that i would write you a few lines to let you know that i am well at present time   i havenot received no leter from you for some time and wish that you would answer my letters

we have a very good plaise for our camp   plenty of to eat and drink and plenty of walnuts to eat   i am as well contented as if i was at home for i have got hardend to the way we live so that i donot care any thing about it   i would just as leave bee in one plaise as a nother and lay down in the dirt as on a feather bed.   that is so we got our rations for two days to day and our meet **(meat)** *-- after we brought it in the tent -- it got up and walked out dorse   I have not anymore to write this time   i hope that this letter will find you all well*

to Dear Mother

H Smith

This letter is hauntingly prophetic of some soldier's feelings well over a century later in Vietnam where they, too, wondered if divisiveness at home might not be the enemy's strongest ally.

November 4, 1863

Dear Friends

We had our lection yester day. and to day we are a quarling be caus this man voted that ticket and he is mad because we voted the true union ticket   Now here is some that is siding for doing harm and here we are fighting for the union   How can we put down this rebelion; when others is a fighting against us in the ranks -- that is what causes the rebels to hang on so long no enemy is a going to quit when they sees we are quarling with ourselves   the way to win is to stand to gether

Now I say let evry man take right hold and stand for the goverment. Here us soldiers here in the army we are fighting and induring the hard times of a soldeers life   why not the sitizens of Wisconsin or any other state stand behind us   must this war last three years longer on a count of the people at home?   now let them come out for the union and sink this rebelion out of existence.

Here is some in the 22 Regt that voted a Democrat ticket. well! they had the pleasure of voting that ticket, and then they had the fun of riding a rail around Camp   that is the way evry man in the north ought to bee served or put in prison with balls and Chains on him   serve him as you would a bushwhacker and then this rebelion will be Crushed in a few months with out any trouble and the union will be restored once more

Harvey Smith

In this letter the good soldier makes a brave show of taking hardship "like a trooper." He then tells a tale of rank insubordination which was near mutiny, which strategem apparently prevailed.

November 19, 1863

Dear Friends

I was glad to receive you letter of the 11th   it came at hand last night and I was glad to hear that you wer all well at present. I am well at present time and have bin for the last two or three weeks and have injoyed myself at the best

It is a raining here to day and has bin all the last two or three last days and it looks like we would have a wet spell   our tents is quite comfertable it leaks a little when it comense to rain   whin it is wet out dourse our going out and in makes the inside of the tent wet   but we do not care anything about it for we are so naturalised to it so it does not go against the grain mutch.

the Tenneseans say that the 22 Regiment is the worst Regiment that ever went along through Tennesey but we do not care   we are going through this state as strate as a bee line and our Colonel sais so   he is not a southern rights man.   This war would come to a close in two months if all the head men was for the union as mutch as our Colonel for he is a man up to the march   som of the head Brigadear Generals is mad at our Colonel because he is a man for the union   they thretend to take him out of the Regiment the other day but we shoulderd arms and told them to try it if they wanted to   and they back down prety quick   and said nothing more about it.

Yesterday the boys brot two southern men up to the General headquaraters blind folded   they wanted a pass to Kentuckey   they blind folded them so that they could not see how we were situated   we suppose they were out as spyes for the rebel army

I have wrote all that I can think of this time. This is to the hole family write all the news if you canot find enough time to write in one day, take tow days

Harvey Smith

To the Family

A lonely soldier makes a humorous, yet pointed, plea for his family to remember him.

December 20, 1863

Mother

I will write you a few lines to let you know that I am well at present and I hope that this may find you well you inquire around there if there is a famly by the name of Smith and if there is a famly by that name tell them to write

Harvey Smith

This letter sums up a soldier's feelings--he extols the cause for which he fights; he expresses loneliness. And, oh, how very real the feelings of this human who died so long ago. He was as much a person as we who read these lines.

March 30, 1864

Dear Friend's

Your letter which was dated the twenty first came to hand to day. I was glad to hear that you are all well and injoying good health. Your letter found me well and injoying as good health as can be expected for the way

125

we have to live; exposed to the stormes and hard times that a soldier has to indure while he is doing the duty that his country calls him to do   that is the way we have to indure hardships and storms of all kinds. But what is the diference as long as it is all for the union   I am willing to do all that I can.

We understand that we are under marching orders now   we think that we are going down the cumberlain river. But we do not know where we will go   that we do not know till we get there

I suppose that the reason for this order is that we understand that old Forest **(Confederate General Nathan Bedford Forest)** *is trying another raid along the railroad as he has tried several time before   they sais he was going up in Kentucky but I guess that he will miss it.*

You said that you had not heard from me for a long time; that is nothing. I think that I have not had a letter from you since we have bin here at nashville till to day   when I get a letter from you I allways answer it as soon as it becomes night so that the camp is still so that I can write without being disturbed and can colect my thoughts together.

I will bring my letter to a close by asking you to excuse all mistakes and poor writing. I like to hear from you as often as you do from me becaus I get lonesom and when I get a letter from you it puts me in good spirets again

Yours truly

Harvey Smith

In this letter, Harvey mentions *dog tents*. These tents were made in two sections. Each man would carry half a tent, and men would pair up to make a complete tent for sleeping. By World War II an even more compact version was in vogue and, naturally, was called a *pup tent*.

April 25, 1864

Dear Friend

I thought that I would write you a few lines this morning to let you know that I am well at the present time and hope that these few lines may find you injoying the same Blessing.

We have a prety good time at the present and I hope we will have good times we expect that the rebels will attack us every day we have these dog tents now that is so two men can sleep in one of them and when we are on a long march we have to cary ar rations for a week We can cary the tents on our backs

I was on guard last night and it rained and was as dark at pitch the rebels could slip up and kil a fellow on his post as well as not but I did not fear them. We are cauled up at three o clock in the morning and stay in line of Battle till sun up and that every morning we sleep with our arms handy so that we can put our hands on them at a minits warning

I will bring my letter to a close by asking you to write soon

From Harvey Smith

This next letter from Harvey is obviously hurried. It reveals a soldier's state of mind on the eve of battle. The next-to-the-last paragraph is garbled; his mind is preoccupied with visions of what the morrow may bring.

127

Mae 2, 1864

Friend at home

As this is the only opportunity that I may have in some time again to write to you I thought that I would improve the present opportunity by writing you a few lines to let you know that I am well and where I am We are camped at the foot of lookout mountain and in the morning we take our position in front and will put up with what may befall us. We are expecting a Battle in a short time and we may be in it

We have bin on the road from nashville to this place thirteen days we have about four day more till we reach Georgia we have to cary evry thing that we take along with us. I have caried all that I have so far and expect to cary it the rest of the time. The officers are to take dog tentes the same as we have had evr since we came to nashville last summer the officers hafto cary evry thing that they have.

I have not much to write to day and I will bring my letter to a close by asking you to write soon and if I and write when I get time I will I expect that there is not much mail that goes to front in such a buisy time as it is now

There is great danger of the mail geting captured Direct by the way of Nashville Tenn 22 Regt wis vol inft Co K

Harvey Smith

Write Soon

The next letter requires no explanation.

May 20, 1864
Division Hospital
near the battle field of Resaca Ga

Mr. Smith

Dear Sir:

This letter is the bearer of sad intelligence to you. Harvey died last night about midnight. He was wounded last Sabbath (May 15) in the fearful charge on a rebel fort. I think he fell about 2 p.m. He was wounded through both legs near the knees. I think the wounds at the time were not considered dangerous, though they were bad. He lingered along in great pain till last night when he passed away. His things have been taken care of by one of his company. Whatever is of any account will probably be forwarded to you. It is indeed sad to see so many of our poor boys dying and dead.

There are about 600 in all in this hospital--or rather have been since the battle of Sunday. The 22d had 10 killed and about 60 wounded, four of whom have since died.

The rebels have been completely routed and are now some 30 miles from here, but our victory has been purchased at a most fearful sacrifice.

The charge we made on the rebel fort was a terrible one. With a wild cry our men pushed forward right up in front of cannon loaded to within six inches of the muzzle. We captured the guns before they could be discharged the last time--4 in number.

We buried your son this morning with the rest who sleep here.

May God in infinite mercy sustain you in this trying ordeal. I trust you have long ere this learned to trust in God.

Yours truly
G.S. Bradley
Chaplain 22d Wis

Following is the pair of letters from Smith's neighbors, relating to Wesley Patton. The first letter is from Wesley. He writes from Camp Randall in Madison, only 30 miles from Brodhead. Wesley's letter reflects his self-acquired education. He wanted to be a physician and was avidly reading books so that he could pass the entrance examination to the university. He died when he was 21. The second letter was written exactly one month later by his best friend, James Vance.

May 6, 1864

Head quarters co. "D"
36" Reg't.

Father,

Yours was gladly recieved. I was glad to here from home but sorry to hear of the sickness of the family. I am well and feel satisfied. I got the appointment of Color Sergeant yesterday. I did not know any thing about it until the colonel called me out of the ranks and, in the presence of the Reg't, he delivered to me the colors of the Reg't accompanied by a soul stirring speech.

It is the most dangerous position in the Reg't., but I would not refuse the appointment, it would have shown cowardice. I will bear that flag to victory, or death

I think I will leave the state about next Tuesday. I do not want any of you to come up here before that time. We have parted once and let that suffice. Vance is with me in all things.

We got the news here that Lee had retreated toward Richmond and that Grant had crossed the Rapidan. There was great rejoicing in the thirty sixth.

I have been drilling in the Barracks this evening so as to be prepared for an examination if I am lucky enough to procure a commission.

Take good care of Buck (**his dog**). *I will come back if the Rebel balls are not too strong for me.*

I think my show is good.

Give my love to Lib and Ruf (**his aunt and uncle**). *I would like to hear from Mother.*

Hoping to hear from you soon, I remain,

Your Son

Wesley W. Patton

The letter which follows was written by Wesley's friend, James Vance.

June 6, 1864   Army of the Potomac

Mr. and Mrs. Patton,

It becomes my painful duty of informing you of your son, Wesley, who was shot Sunday June 5th at about 10 O'clock A.M. The wound was mortal. He died at 10:30 P.M. I was with him from the time he was shot until he was buried. He suffered much pain but bore it like a soldier.

We buried him decently, placed a board with his name, day of death, age and Reg't to his grave, that he may be found at any time should you come to move him. I tried all I could to send his body home and the Sargent tried but could not do it. The place of his burrial is Cold Harbor, Virginia.

He was in his right mind until his last moments and talked a bout his friends and relations, but we could not convince him he must die. He talked with the minister and said he put all his trust in his savior, hoped his parents prayed for his redemption. He died without a struggle, I wiped the cold clammy sweat off his fair brow, while the cold hand of death was doing its mission.

Oh what a loss it is to us, we would rather lose any other than Wesley. Twice, did he bear our banner through the thick ravages of battle, but at last did his manly form fall as the mighty oak beneath the tempest. Wesley was brave, he feared not danger, he was liked by all the regiment.

I am well and healthy but my pleasures are ended since Wesley is no more. Mourn not his loss because the Nations homage does him honor for his bravery.

So no more at present but Remain your reverent friend.

Sympathies,

James P. Vance

The loss of sons was a deep and abiding tragedy for the Smith and Patton families. Over 600,000 other American families suffered the loss of their sons, too. The war had killed roughly one person out of every thirty across the entire population. The percentage of deaths among young adult males was noticeably high.

An entire generation would pass before America smiled again. Music, for example, would not regain its spirit and liveliness until the advent of "ragtime" in the 1890s.

With the conclusion of the Civil War, the stage was set for a new era in the life of the Smith family.

CHAPTER SIX

THE TURN OF THE CENTURY, 1880-1919

The Smiths were fortunate in 1875 to have a fourth child. Hannah was 35 and Francis was 51 when daughter Addie entered their lives. Almost immediately the Smiths began plans for their dream home. They moved into it in 1877 and placed their collection of family keepsakes in the attic. Their ancestors had been "savers," too, and some of the items dated to the American Revolution--1775--and before. The plain wooden pioneer trunks which had made the trek west from New York in the 1850's were retained and became the repository for future family treasures.

In a world in which cheap entertainments and trivial pursuits were virtually non-existent, the family was the center of individual lives. Having lost three children already, the Smiths lavished more than an ample measure of love and affection upon Addie. Parenting was a refined art then, and Addie grew up to be as good a human being as society can create.

The definitive character sketch of Addie relates the tale of the worst thing she ever did in her life--being late for school one morning when she was six! The fateful drama begins with her departure for school one morning when she was in the first grade. She hugged her mother goodbye at the back door and began the five-block walk to school. The school was on the same street as Smith's house, and the arrow-straight route was one which any child could follow. But after a block, Addie got a better idea. She decided to jog over one block and follow the paralleling railroad track. The stroll along the track proved to be interesting enough. It was then that the six-year-old noticed a distinct humming sound emanating from a telegraph pole. She pressed her ear to the pole and was mesmerized. Then and there she decided to listen to every pole along her route.

The upshot was that Addie was nearly a half hour late for school. For the rest of her life she would recall that event in the privacy of her family, always concluding the tale with the hope that none of the children from her class remembered the incident into adulthood and thought her to be an irresponsible person for it. Living to age 74, Addie never lost her self-control to the extent that she used such irreverent language as *hell* or *damn*. She never gambled, never smoked, never tasted an alcoholic beverage, and never kissed a man other than the one she married.

In the nineteenth century internal cancer was not treatable, and Francis contracted cancer of the colon. He died a slow, painful death and was gone at age 60. Hannah and Addie were left with the arduous task of earning an income. The world of 1882 pretty much defined women as not being wage earners. They had rental income from the Main Street store and from its upstairs apartment. They rented two upstairs bedrooms to "boarders" and prepared their meals. And, Hannah did other people's laundry for pay.

One bright spot on Hannah and Addie's financial horizon was Uncle Al in New York City. There he owned a department store and apartment houses. Without a family of his own, he pledged to leave his fortune to Hannah and Addie. When Al died during Addie's high school years, his lawyers notified Hannah that his estate had no money left after paying expenses. Hannah and Addie took that statement at face value. One might wonder if that really was the truth.

Two years after the death of Francis Smith, Hannah married Will Hyde. Addie again had a devoted father-figure. A wealthy southern land owner, Mr. Hyde had lost wife, seven children, property, and money to the ravages of the Civil War. Starting life anew as a northerner, he worked sometimes at printing presses, sometimes as an auctioneer, and most of the time as a traveling salesman. Indeed, he was absent from Brodhead over half the time. As he struggled with heavy sample cases on and off trains at his frequent stops, he must have mused at how fickle the winds of fortune can blow.

In 1893 Addie was one of 15 students to graduate from Brodhead High School. She delivered a beautiful commencement address which appears among this chapter's letters. The ties to home were too strong to permit her to forge the teaching career she thought she wanted, and she settled into domestic life with her mother and step-father.

In only a year conditions changed again. One spring evening at supper time, Mr. Hyde went to the back porch to get a pitcher of water from the pump. Upon returning, he was unable to open the door; then unable to stand. He had "suffered some form of paralysis," they said at the time. Today we would call it a stroke. He promptly died. In his vest pocket was the small photograph of a woman unknown to Hannah and Addie. Was it his first wife? If so, no harm. Or, was it a current lover? Being absent from Brodhead more than he was present, he could have been living a double life. Hannah and Addie always wondered.

Then, at the turn of the century Loudon Blackbourne strode into Addie's life. Twenty-one, standing six-foot-two and a dapper dresser, he was strikingly handsome. With only an eighth-grade education, he had continued to educate himself. His grammar was impeccable and he possessed the manners of an aristocrat. Smiling, good-natured and an outstanding singer, he even belonged to Addie's church. He was precisely what she needed.

During their courtship, Addie would light a kerosene lamp and place it next to the electric lamp. The city fathers had decreed that all decent folk would have no need of electricity after 9 PM, and the power plant shut down at that hour. Addie didn't want Loudon to leave at nine, and with the kerosene lamp lit she reasoned he wouldn't notice when the electric light went out. One of the original electric light bulbs was in the attic-- still in working order--and it is, indeed, no brighter than a kerosene lamp.

On a Sunday afternoon drive, Loudon stopped the carriage inside the locally famous covered bridge which spanned the Sugar River and proposed marriage. That Monday Addie and Loudon rode the cars--well, by then it was called the "train"--to Monroe to buy their marriage license.

Addie and Loudon were married in 1906 and had daughter Rosamond in 1909 and daughter Joyce in 1910. Addie was four years older than Loudon, and she was not the stunning "looker" he was. But, she was the kind of woman he needed for a wife. She was devoted and shared all his basic values. With the marriage, Loudon became the "man of the house" in Hannah and Addie's home--his dream home since the first time he saw it. And, he acquired the rights to occupy their store building. Loudon was poised for his first fling with the world of business.

The letters of the era follow. By now envelopes are of standard sizes. Both conventional stamps and postage-printed envelopes are in use, as are modern-style postal cancellation marks. Addresses are still simple two-liners: merely the person's name and city.

During the era of this chapter the first attempts were made to standardize letter format and punctuation. An early attempt to standardize the punctuation following a salutation was the use of a colon followed by a hyphen. This oddity prevailed for about 25 years and is evident in some of the letters in this chapter.

A LIVELY SCENE IN CHURCH—Some wicked wretch turned a three-foot snake loose in Olive Branch Church last night during services, and the scene that followed beggars description. The ladies gathered their skirts up around them and climbed upon the chairs or else rushed frantically towards the door and escaped into outer darkness. The crawling thing was finally killed and quiet restored. The perpetrator of the cruel joke is unknown.—*Indianapolis News*

Advertisement from Francis Smith's store. An interesting news item appears in the next column.

By 1881 Francis was suffering with cancer, with a year to live. He made several trips to Chicago to visit a cancer specialist. Here his 43-year-old wife writes a letter of loving concern. Six-year-old daughter, Addie, is mentioned.

Hannah signs her name, "Rie." She went by that name which was derived from her middle name. She was born "Hannah Maria Allen." She had attended the first grade for only three weeks when her father concluded that the family couldn't afford to do without her physical labor at home. Later she taught herself to read and write, but never had the chance to really master these skills which people of the twentieth century take for granted.

August 27, 1881   Brodhead, Wisconsin

My Dear Husband

I have been thinking about you so strong that I can hardly know what I am doing   I have just got your nice letter and I was so glad to hear from you again   You dont know how much good it does me to hear from you.

I think of you all of the time   I follow you in my mind down town and back every day and wish I was there to have dinner with you and to hold you at night   Addie has gone to bed & She say to tell you that she ate so much fish she couldnt write and will write those letters tomorrow

now you must feel the best you can and not get discourged   I believe you will get well   The Church **(one which she could see across the street)** *has had lecture every night this week and the meeting is just out with a good crowd a leaving*

Mr Stackings Boy that was taken Sick last May is dead after so much suffering   I dont know as there is any more news to write this time

a kiss from Addie Bell and me and a good lot of love from your Wife Rie

good bye until Sunday

In the summer of 1888, when Addie was about to begin eighth grade, she and her mother made a trip to New York. They visited relatives in Grafton, Troy, and New York City. The greatest marvel of their adventure was the brand new Statue of Liberty. Thirteen-year-old Addie preserved her impressions of the visit in writing; and in subsequent years, relegated the paper to one of the attic trunks. It's a delightful child's insight into the America of 1888.

August 24, 1888   New York City

Our train brought us to New York yesterday morning. After a day of getting settled at our hotel and resting up--this morning we took the street cars to Battery Park. There we purchased tickets for the harbor ships. We made our way to the docking place and the crowd was fierce. After dodging carriages and ducking under horses heads we joined the throng at the waters edge.

After a time one sighted a great ship and inquired if that were ours. "No!" came a reply "that is the hospital ship where people with dangerous illness are quarantined." Before long came the shout "Here is our ship". We boarded and began our trip in the great harbor. We sailed past docks crowded with the merchant ships of many nations. We passed the great forts whose silent guns signal a warning to any nation which would attempt to place us in servitude.

Then a silence came over the ship as all crowded the rails in breathless wonder and awe at the magnificence of the great lady of liberty shining in the morning sun.

In one of Paul Davidson's letters in the 1850s he mentioned that Ira Allen had become owner of a lumber yard in Troy, New York. Ira was Hannah's brother. Now, roughly 40 years later, he has died. The news comes to Hannah in a letter from her sister Ette.

November 5, 1889   Troy, New York

Dear Sister Rie,

Of course you have or will receive notice of Ira's death. He was at the "Yard" Monday but was distressed. He was suffering for want of breath. He could not sleep that night. Tuesday he did not go down to the yard. He walked the floor most of the day.

Al **(Ira's son)** *came home and wanted him to have some eminent physician examine him. Ira insisted that money not be wasted on such a thing. Miss Harris the lady that keeps the house did all that could be done for him.*

At 12.30 past noon he was sitting in his chair   said he "felt strange" straightened back and was gone.

I was as Stroudsburg Pennsylvania. Had been there six days. went for a rest and a change. received dispatch **(telegram)** *and started in 30 minutes. I'll always regret that I was not there to do what I could for him. I know that he would have appreciated it. I saw him a week before I went away and was shocked at the change. he looked so haggared, had lost 25 lbs.*

With love and sympathy from us all,

Your affectionate sister,

Ette

Four days later, Ette writes to Hannah again. This letter bears the details of Ira's funeral. It also reveals the fact that Ira had paid for Hannah's and Addie's trip to New York the previous summer, and that his stingy daughter, Jenny, will now find out when she sees the cancelled checks. In leaving over $100,000 to each of his children, Ira's estate was worth many millions in 1999 dollar values.

139

November 9, 1889   New York City

Dear sister Rie,

Yours rec'd hope you are better. The funeral at Central Church was largely attended with scores of business men some from Troy being present. Eight of his old friends acted as pall bearers.

We went from the Church to Central Station to take cars for Norwich to attend the Episcopal service at the house. We were all dumbfounded on reaching the house to find Jenny in such good spirits. Al broke down on meeting her in the hall. She was all smiles and said, "Al, don't be silly" in her high pitched tone. And to the rest of us, "How sweet of you to come. I don't want anyone to be sad or show any sign of grief. I want you to have a nice time." She was jolly.

Jenny may feel badly, but I don't think she shed a tear. Her grief has apparently been recompensed by the money she will get, which will probably amount to more than $100,000.00. She was too stingy to send carriages to take us to the house. It would have cost one dollar more. She wanted a cheaper casket. Al said <u>no</u> most emphatically and got one that cost $125.

But Jenny was able to spend money on herself alright. She wore a black lace dress, astrakhan cape, black hat, and black velvet gloves. They went nicely with her high toned airs. I told her I thought her mothers ashes should be put beside him. She did not think it made any difference. I suppose she will see the check stub sometime and know how you came **(who paid for the trip)** *last summer.*

Al feels terribly blue. He thinks he must step into Ira's shoes immediately, and yet knows nothing about the business.

I feel with you that we have lost a dear brother, and will remember all his good qualities for he certainly was a good brother.

In heartfelt sympathy

Your loving sister   Ette

140

In 1890 Addie was ending her Freshman year at Brodhead High School. She won the school-wide essay contest which was held to name a student to speak at the Memorial Day service. She won with a poem which she delivered to the crowd gathered at the end of the parade route in the South Side Park.   Addie's intellectual advancement is noticeable in the two years since she wrote about the Statue of Liberty.

Memorial Day in 1890 was, of course, one of THE community events of the year. The nation still enjoyed some of the revolutionary spirit from its founding, and society was absolutely consumed with remembrances of the Civil War which had ended a mere 25 years earlier. In small-town America, Memorial Day 1890 was attended by virtually every able-bodied citizen. In Brodhead they listened to a young lady.

We Deck Their Graves Alike To-Day

We deck their graves alike to-day,
With blossoms fresh and fair,
And on the grassy mounds of clay,
We lay the flow'rs with care.
As o'er each sleeping hero's head,
Our offerings are placed,
The brav'ry of our honored dead,
Shall never be erased.

We deck their graves alike to-day,
With springtime's fairest flow'rs,
And now and then the songster's play
Makes bright the solemn hours.
The violet and lilac sweet,
Or wreath of evergreen,
At every soldier's head and feet,
Memorial Day is seen.

We deck their graves alike to-day,
And raise our anthems high,
For those who fell when far away,
Beneath a distant sky.
Our Country called her gallant sons,
For service in the fray,
And on the graves of fallen ones
We'll strew sweet flow'rs today.

This letter finds Hannah's generation continuing to dwindle in number.

April 28, 1891   Bath on the Hudson, New York

Dear Sister Rie

Your Brotherinlaw Charles Smith died monday night, 25 minutes to Eleven o clock of a stroke. Mrs. Smith and him went to Berlin three weeks ago last friday and going from the depot to where I live he stubed his toe and got a hard fall. it broke his shoulder and threw his arm out of place.

Since then he had a shock of peralises on his left side and could not stir or help him Self the lest bit till he died. the neighbors has been with Mrs. Smith that she would not be alone

from your sister ever

Eveline

This letter from Hannah (she calls herself *Maria* or *Rie*) was written to Addie while she was visiting a friend in Janesville between her Junior and Senior years of high school. Hannah sounds like something of an old lady, though she is in her fifties. She uses the phrase, "digging out," meaning "to feel better." And, she tells the tale of the great lightning strike--a story which was still being repeated among the family 60 years later.

142

June 24, 1892   Brodhead, Wisconsin

My Dear Daughter

I just thought you would like to get one word from home   We are all well I have put in a good deal of my time over to the Drs but have not been over there yet today   I have been digging out a little **(feeling better)**

well I dont know how it has been out there where you are, but we have had some of the hardest storms that I ever Saw   The one on Wensday night was just terrible   it Struck our Electric wire and burned out the plug up stairs and came down in the sitting Room and Burned the wire off in two places   There was a Ball of fire went over Toby **(a cat)** *and under the Dining room Table   it made Toby jump and shout I tell you   it was befor Pa got home about half past Six*

Will Stevenson was coming from Albany in a buggy   the lightning Struck in the field and Scorched him So that two Dr had to work over him all night   he was unconsious up to noon the next day   think he is better now

have a good time down to Jennies   I will be at the ten o clock train on Monday to meet you   So good bye untill I See you from your loveing Mama to her darling Daughter Addie

Maria Hyde

Mr. Hyde saved this letter which Hannah wrote to him while he was on a business trip to Marengo, Iowa. This is the first letter in the collection to be written with a pencil, all previous ones having been in ink. The fountain pen was invented in the 1880s; we can be certain that all prior letters were written with quill pens or dip-in-ink steel-pointed pens.

May 1, 1893   Brodhead, Wisconsin

My Dear Husband

I rec your letter of the 29 this morning So will anser right away

*well to day is like all of the rest we have had for the last two weeks --
rainy and cloudy   do hope the Sun has not left us for good but it looks
like it has   if we could have some bright days so the leaves could start
out I should be so glad to see them   there does not anything grow here
but the grass and that not very fast   the buds on the trees look just as they
did three weeks ago*

*am very glad to hear that your toe is better   Addie seems to be on the
gain now   Will Schemp is sick in bed I hear but dont know how bad he is
so hope it is nothing serious   Mrs Sydman is up tearing around* **(being
very active)** *as of old you would not think she had ever been sick*

will close with love from Addie and my Self from you loveing Wife

Maria Hyde

**Addie Smith graduated from Brodhead High School in the spring of
1893 when she was 18 years old. High school graduation in the 1890s
was less common than college graduation in the 1990s. Attendance
was voluntary, and less than ten percent of the high-school-age
population chose to attend. Scholarship was rigorous; standards were
high. One of Addie's teachers from Brodhead High School--a Mr.
McGovern--went on to become governor of the state. Addie's
daughters, Rosamond and Joyce, graduated from the University of
Wisconsin in Madison a generation later and felt that their mother's
high school education was comparable to theirs from the University.
They sometimes posed the question, "I wonder what Mamma would
have become professionally if she'd gone to college?"**

**At the graduation ceremony, Addie delivered the commencement
address (using the generic *men* where we might now say *people*).**

Hannah with daughter, Addie, in the 1890s. Their attire is one bit of evidence which might prompt an observer of the American scene to call the 1890s, "The most civilized decade."

Monuments Not of Stone

Great men, great deeds, great events are commemorated 'round the world in monuments which are intended to endure, so that the greatness not be lost, but rather be an inspiration for generations yet unborn. These monuments we can see. Great pyramids by the Nile, the pillars of Thebes, the columns and arches and monoliths of Rome are monuments which have endured. In our own land in any park you may see cannon commemorating battles, Grant on a horse, or Lincoln seated in a chair. These are great monuments for great men and their deeds.

What of ordinary men? Are great monuments ever in store for them? Who builds a great dome of granite and brass to the mother who teaches her children the Golden Rule? Who raises a marble obelisk to the clerk who gives honest measures at the scale?

Ask again, why monuments are raised. The answer: that greatness not be lost, that honest deeds endure, that future generations emulate deeds well done. Here is the supreme measure of equality. All men--all men from the greatest to the least--have equal opportunity to live life well. Every man has equal chance to live out the Scriptural admonition, "So let your light shine before men that they will see your good works and glorify your Father which is in Heaven."

The monument which every man is free to build is the monument of his good name. His monument is his reputation and the example he sets. His monument is those things he teaches to his children. These are the things that endure; the things which live after. In time stone will crumble and metal will tarnish or rust, and these things will fall away. An example well set and a lesson well taught can live forever if generations to come are faithful to the quest.

The greatest monuments are not monuments of stone. The greatest monuments are the monuments of the human heart which neither moth nor rust, nor rot, nor fire can ever diminish. Build a monument of heart, mind, and soul in whose light future generations will find their way. After the work of the ages is done, it will be seen that ordinary men have built the greatest monuments of all--monuments not of stone.

Now in the autumn of 1893 Addie is in her first year out of high school. In September she had her three-week experiment with school teaching, and now she and her mother are enjoying an extended visit with relatives in New York. Mr. Hyde writes from a hotel in Glenwood, Iowa, to his wife in Grafton, New York.

Note that in this letter Mr. Hyde hyphenates *to-day*. This is an evolutionary half step between the two-word *to day* which prevailed in earlier letters and the compound word *today* of the twentieth century. A great many common words followed this evolutionary pattern at the same time; among them *percent, tomorrow, anything, picnic,* and *alright.*

November 24, 1893   Glenwood, Iowa

My Dear Wife:-

I received your letter of the 16th addressed to this place, to-day. I am very sorry you are in bad health and it worries me. I don't think it is good for you to be out there in New York -- But I can't be at home to stay with you until February, and then I will have to be away during the month of April.

Tell Addie "Daddy loves her" and that I want to see her quite as bad as she wants to see me. I want to see you still more

I am taking a 250 dollar order to-day, and shall be in Atlantic to spend Sunday. Write me at Marengo, Iowa at Ketchum House -- I don't know where to address this letter but will try East Grafton. I am feeling first rate to-day and hope you are improving.

I am your loving husband

Will

This letter from Will Hyde to his wife Hannah expresses some of the rigors of being a traveling salesman in the 1890s.

December 9, 1893   Ainsworth, Iowa

My dear Wife

I shall send by Express to-morrow sixty dollars to you at South Berlin, N. Y. in currency -- I shall also write to Jim Terry in Brodhead to buy 2 tons of coal and I will go home between the 15th and 20th and get the house warm for you. I shall send the money from Columbus, Ia.

I am completely tired out and my back aches fearfully, for I have stood over my sample trunks 4 and 5 hours every day this week but I shall get to Columbus Ia to-night and will take a good rest until Monday morning. I shal have to come back in January for I am not near through, but I have written so many letters that customers are waiting for me till January.

Love to Addie

Hoping to see you soon I am as ever

Will

In the spring of 1894 Will Hyde passed away. Now it is the end of August. Addie is visiting a friend in Fort Atkinson, Wisconsin. Hannah has a teenage girl named Cecie staying with her to help with housework and to provide company. Hannah is now 54, but considers herself old. Since age 50 she spends much time in a rocking chair with a black shawl draped around her shoulders. It's been a hard life, and she is typical of her generation.

Hannah mentions going riding, and one might conjure up an image of a woman astride a horse. It is doubtful that ladies of Hannah's ilk ever did that; the ride was certainly in a carriage *behind* the horse.

August 21, 1894   Brodhead, Wisconsin

My Dear Daughter Addie

I was So pleased to get your letter last night.

148

well I went a riding last night and took Mrs. Ballou   to-night I took Mrs Stewart   if nothing happens I will take Mrs Sydman to-morrow

The Congregational Sunday School had a picnic on the church lawn to day   The Parsonage is nearly Painted and it looks quite nice

Jim Broughton is in town a visiting.   He stopped to see me and I asked to what I owed the honor of his visit.   He said his mother gave him a list of the names of the old women she would like him to call on and away he went straight to see me.

Cecie told me to tell you that She and I had a nine o clock tea last night and then the band played **(in the park a block away)** *and we marched to the Barn with a pail of water for Flora* **(the horse)**   *So dont you think we are having a good time   so you can stay just as long as you want to*

Dr. Bennetts daughter was married.   Cecie came home with fruit and cake from the wedding for me   the Dr had fourteen extra Electric lights put in the house for the event   Mrs Bennett gave her a very handsome silver tea set and a very handsome butter knife   Ralf Bement gave her a nice Silver Spoon and Carrie Englebritson gave her China Sugar and Creamer   her father gave her a five dollar gold piece and Mr Stevenson gave them each a one hundred dollar Bill

Cecie is a **(in)** *bed   So I guess that I will go too*

from your loving Mother

H M Hyde

This letter from Hannah to Addie was written just three days after the previous one.   It's just a brief letter of small-talk, but reveals something of the personality of the writer.

August 24, 1894   Brodhead, Wisconsin

My Dear Daughter Addie

I got your letter to night so will write a little to you. I think you should go the depot and get that return ticket made for any day you want to come home. You don't have to come home as soon as the date on the ticket. They can change it to any day you please.

now Addie dont come home untill you get your visit out of you Stay all next week   I am a getting along all right   of course I shall be glad to See you when you come but dont hury on my account   Cecie Stays with me every night and I dont get near as lonely as I thought that I would

give my love to them all   write when you will come so I can be at the train to meet you

I do not think of any thing more to write so I bid you a good night

from

your loving Mother

Mrs H M Hyde

Now comes the first letter from the collection of Loudon Blackbourne. (Just as various members of the Davidson family wrote their name with or without the medial *d*, so various Blackbournes wrote their name with or without the terminal *e*.) This letter is from 1895 before Loudon and Addie have met. But, it is a letter which he kept and it eventually made its way to the attic in Smith's house. Loudon was 16 when he received this letter, and was still a lad at home on the farm. Quite possibly, this is the first letter he ever received.

Loudon was one of six children. Loudon's family letters in the collection are from his father, Fred; his brother, Fred; and from his sister, Mary. This first letter is from Mary. She was his favorite

member of the family, and unfortunately she died of tuberculosis when in her thirties. News which she found to be perfectly serious has been rendered quite hilarious by the passage of time.

Mary has taken their mother to a hot springs resort in Indiana--quite a trip at the time from their farm home in Dunbarton, Wisconsin. The resort's letterhead includes the following claims:

The beneficial effects of the water and magnetic mud of the Indiana Mineral Springs has been proven in the cure of rheumatism, dyspepsia, and almost every other form of disease. The Hunter House is located on the summit of the hill from which the spring flows. The spring water has the most pronounced diuretic and alterative effects of any, especially when used in connection with the magnetic mud which environs it. Good cooks and attentive servants do all that can be done for the comfort of the guests. The Hunter hack meets all trains. Rates are $2 per day or $10 per week.

August 14, 1895   Indiana Mineral Springs P.O., Indiana

Dear Brother Loudon:

Rec'd your letter last night and will answer this morning   It is just half past eight o'clock and Ma is just getting in the mud   I will hav a little while to write while she is in there but then I will have to dress her

I told ma that you asked me if the men handled the women down here & if they stripped them off naked -- and we had such a big laugh over it. No! Loudon they have ladies to handle the ladies and gents for gents.

They have a pond here and I heard there was fish in it so I went and threw in some crackers. My how thick they come up to eat--you would like to see them. If you ever come here bring a hook and some line with you.

I dont know how long it will take this cure to help Ma with her rheumatism but I think it will take a mighty long time. You would laugh if you could see them Loudon for it does look very funny to see all these people sitting in mud. Ma is to stay in the mud about half an hour. then she goes in a shower bath and then to a hot room where she is to stay until she quits sweating and Ma can sweat for a long time. From there she goes to the bath tub. then I have to put a gown on her and roll her to our room in a wheel chair and then change her clothes. It takes until nearly noon to get through all this and dressed for dinner

With love to all I bid you Good bye until the next time

Lovingly Mary

In 1897 Loudon Blackbourne is a young man of 18, living and working in Darlington, Wisconsin. In this letter, brother Joe Blackbourne's wife, Nellie, writes to say that Joe has left her. It must have come as quite a blockbuster of a letter, for divorce was almost unheard of at the time and Loudon was still young and impressionable.

Joe and Nellie had met when Joe was 17 and he had decided to go to the school house after hours for private tutoring to further his education which had ended when he was 13. Nellie was the teacher, and she was 20. They fell in love, married, and within a few years the lad had second thoughts.

This letter shows Nellie to be truly caring and magnanimous under the circumstances, and this reveals her character. Subsequent to the letter, Joe and Nellie did divorce. Later they married others. Joe had a long and happy marriage, and several children, with his second wife. Seemingly a lifetime later, Joe and Nellie lost their spouses; and, astonishingly, were remarried to each other on the fiftieth anniversary of their divorce! They lived to be in their nineties.

Joe and his twin sister, Maggie, were annually featured in the leading state newspapers during the early 1960s as the oldest twins living in Wisconsin.

Mr. Loudon Blackbourn.

Dear Loudon.

You and I have always been friends haven't we? Oh Loudon I am going to try your friendship now as I never expected to. Joe has gone, Loudon, and none of us know where. He brought his things down to Dunbarton Tues. while I was over at Jesse's **(another brother of Loudon)**. *I didn't know he had really gone until last night. Jess and Ella brought me over home Tues. night and stayed all night. He didn't come home that night nor the next day, so Jess went to Dunbarton to see where he was and Mother told him he had gone. I stayed with your folks last night and am going to South Wayne this morning to see what my people think best to do.*

Later. The train came and I had to stop writing. I am at my folks home now.

Oh Loudon, I don't want to lose your friendship but I do want to know how Retta **(Joe's former girlfriend)** *takes the news and if you think she will go where he is. Won't you, for the sake of old times, write and tell me anything you think I would want to know. If you will write and sort of keep me posted, I shall be ten thousand times obliged and will be glad to serve you in any way in my power.*

I don't know yet what I shall do. For the present I expect to be here at South Wayne.

I take this privilege with you because you have always befriended me and have seemed like a brother to me. I don't have hard feelings toward him. I am sorry for him. You must join with me, Loudon, in praying that he will keep out of bad company and keep himself unspotted from the world. I did love him, Loudon, and I don't want any harm to come to him. I don't want anyone to say bad things about him.

I settled it with the Lord last night, and if God sees fit to bring Joe back

Loudon Blackbourne at the time he moved to Brodhead, Wisconsin.

and make him the husband he promised to be, I shall be glad and happy. If not, I can only say, "Thy will be done."

I am your loving sister,

Nellie B.

Dissatisfied that he never completed the eighth grade, at age 20 Loudon has taken tests at the Shullsburg school to qualify for a grade school diploma. It was something of a "big deal" at the time, as a smaller portion of society finished grade school then than finishes high school now. Loudon was an avid reader and superb conversationalist, and made a lifetime practice of learning all he could on his own.

April 24, 1899   Shullsburg, Wisconsin

Mr. Loudon Blackbourn

My dear Friend:- I take pleasure in notifying you of your successful completion of the examination for a Common School Diploma.

The following are your standings in the several branches:

Physiology	*73*
Geography	*70*
Arithmetic	*70*
Reading	*95*
Grammar	*90*
Orthography	*81*
Constitutions	*70*
U. S. History	*89*
Penmanship	*80*

I am Yours cordially

J. H. Nattrass, Supt

Loudon and Addie Blackbourne are newlyweds in 1906. They are pictured with Loudon's parents, Fred and Victoria, on the front porch of their home in Dunbarton, Wisconsin.

At age 21 Loudon has come to Brodhead. His courtship of Addie has been successful, albeit protracted, and the couple married. Soon after the wedding, Loudon and Addie have gone to Dunbarton to visit Loudon's parents. The preceding photo shows the four of them seated on the porch of the senior Blackbourne's home.

Dunbarton, by the way, is on Brodhead's railway line and it is the sixth depot to the west--approximately 40 miles.

This letter is written to Loudon and Addie while they are in Dunbarton. It is from Addie's mother, Hannah. This letter is first in the collection to use printed stationery, though the quality of both print and paper gives the impression of cheap wallpaper.

September 1, 1906   Brodhead, Wisconsin

Dear Children

I just got your postal   I think it very pretty   had been thinking that you would like to hear from home   I thought I would look in the little Box on the desk here and found this lovely paper   So here goes

everything is all right   folks (**Brodhead residents**) *have most all gone off to Janesville   it is very quiet and we have had little trade* (**few customers in the store**) *it is dull when they all gone to a Circus*

am glad you are having a good time   dont get Sick   Green (**the store clerk**) *just Said "tell them we are having a good time selling wall paper"*

remember me to Mr and Mrs Blackbourne   it is kind of lonesome at the House   Shall be glad to see you both back again

with very much love to you both I remain your Mother

H M Hyde

Addie and Loudon have settled into a pattern of domestic tranquility with Hannah. Loudon is selling wallpaper over the same store counter where Francis Smith once traded with Indians. The Brodhead of 1908 looks pretty much the same as the Brodhead of a decade or score of years earlier. A drastic transformation in the face of civilization is just around the corner.

This letter from Loudon's father, Fred, provides interesting insight into the life of the owner of a small farm and cheese factory in Wisconsin's past when more people lived on farms than in towns and there were more cows than people in the state.

Fred arrived in the United States at age ten, and in the company of two older brothers. They had worked their way on a ship from England to New Orleans; then worked their way up the Mississippi to Galena, Illinois where they headed north. They entered Wisconsin on foot, penniless, each with a small bag of possessions. Fred carried a memento of England, a wooden pepper shaker which ultimately became Loudon's. It was 1840, and only by dint of the hardest work and the shrewdest money management did Fred Blackbourne come to own farm and factory, and have enough money to pay for the local church building.

Fred is a bright man, but from the letter it is evident that he has had little education--perhaps comparable schooling to Hannah's three weeks, perhaps none at all. The turn of the century is an interesting era of letter-writing, because there is such a drastic difference in communication ability between the older generation and their children. That was no doubt *the* era in American history which witnessed the greatest change in educational opportunity from one generation to the next. In the late twentieth century which enjoys compulsory education, communication ability may be taken as a measure of other abilities; but such extrapolations are not valid for people who had no educational opportunities.

Fred is 78, and he writes a letter describing some of the day-to-day happenings of his world.

January 28, 1908   Dunbarton, Wisconsin

Dear son & Daughter & ma Hide

I recived your letter of the 22 yesterday as Ma & I was coming home from Taylors   we had bin visiting their and as we wer coming home it snowed in blizard fashion

I rec'd your letter & left it sitting in the buggy till after I had don the chores   there was a cheese maker drove up to see me as I was backing up the buggy in the shead   he came from wardsville looking to see our factrys and how we do here   I went around with him to talk to the people in the factrys

Fred and Perigo **(Fred's namesake son and his father-in-law)** *are diggin west of the Barn in the Pasture*

I have just got in from dehorning 5 steers & one Heffer   had no bother **(Meaning "no trouble" with the animals which naturally do not take kindly to having their horns removed)** *ma has just churned   has some Butter milk in a Pan on the floor for the dog   now she is washing the churn with boiling water   the Potatoes are cooking for diner*

we are usely well   we are selling our cheese for 13cts when we can get it! have not a great many left   sold some at Kansas city   do you know of any unmarried or single man that can make cheese that wants a job next year

I indorsed the note $108 & hav writen you a receipt for same & will in close it in this letter. if you can pay cash for your goods now I think you will make a store ceeper **(storekeeper)** *all O K   I should judge you could make a lot that way*

Gilbert Shoalls is working Frank vanvoorhis farm   I hear he is going to bach **(live alone as a bachelor)** *for his girl has gone back on him* **(ended their relationship)** *Joe is a diggin an outhouse pit*

my love to you all   your father F Blackbourn

The next pair of letters were written on the same day by Loudon's parents, Victoria and Fred Blackbourne (Loudon's generation spelled the name with an *e*; the older generation did not).

March 5, 1911   Dunbarton, Wisconsin

Dear Son and Daughter

We red your letter on the noon Train and was glad to hear from you   this is a cold windy morning   it might snow   the renter Just got the Chores don

I am glad you are going to have some help in the Store again   Our renter has shipped their goods on the train   it does seam rather still now they are gon

I guess you will be glad when the babys Colic is done **(the first reference to daughter, Joyce, born in 1910)**.

what Eggs are worth is 14 cts   here it is raining a little this morning   Em has a man to work for her and he lives in the cook house at Ems other place

Joe just went Past   they come over nearly every night to meeting **(church)** *he has a fine horse*

Victoria

This letter from Fred Blackbourne mentions someone "having an axe to grind." This phrase has become such a common euphemism for "having a complaint" that it is humorous to see the phrase intended literally.

March 5, 1911   Dunbarton, Wisconsin

Dear Loudon & Family

it is raining with a strong East wind   Your ma & I are a lone & all still in the House save the wind wistling and the clock ticking   the Preacher

& wife was here yesterday making a call but your ma was out & did not git back till after they left

Freds children was hear last night helping your ma catch C.K.s **(chickens?)** *I think your ma & the children caught 73   I told your ma that she Ought to give the rest of the children Each the same*

Pat Lauregan wants to sel his House & lot for $850.00

the Preacher & wife are just coming down the South hill for Sunday School Preaching

My hands are cold though my feet are in the oven & I am near the stove as I can well git **(it was common for people to warm their feet on the open door of the oven of a wood-burning stove).**

my hired man Rob was not up hear very Early this morning & Cy went out & done some of the chores   this is the 2nd day with his wife here   So I blame her for his being late

I see Joe and Tress **(Joe's second wife)** *just coming down the Hill with one Horse & Buggy   they dont miss these meetings   you see I think he thinks he is Serving God by so doing*

I am glad you have enough to ceep you buisy & that Rosamon is a cuet child & Growing fast   so Joice is still in trubble with akes & pains   is she Good looking.   how is Addie & ma Hide   do thay ceep so buisy that thay dont have a word to say to any one but the children & you   I hope thay are well

Oh but it is raining now again

Jesse **(Loudon's brother)** *was hear yesturday with a ax to grind so I went down to the grinding stone with my ax & we changed work   I held his ax on the stone till it was sharp and then got my ax on the stone & ground it a while   finily he said he was in a hurry and wanted to git home and would come another day to help me grind mine   I told him to go then*

with love   your Father   Fred

A dapper 33-year-old Loudon and wife, Addie, are enjoying the prime of life. Grandma Hannah, well worn by her 75 years, has outlived three children and two husbands. For Rosamond and Joyce, the great adventure called "life" is only just beginning.

This letter is written on a sheet of invoice paper from Fred Blackbourne's Dunbarton Cheese Company. At the time Fred is past 80 and Loudon is past 30. Loudon's wallpaper store must not be doing fantastically well, as Loudon is accepting a sizable (for the times) amount of money from his father.

It is interesting that Loudon's letter was received in Dunbarton the same day it was mailed from Brodhead. The two towns were half-a-dozen station stops from each other on the same rail line, and the railroad operated a Railway Post Office car in which mail was sorted en route.

Fred's letter shows affection for the ladies in his life, and reveals a bit of his sense of humor. Most of all, the letter reveals the labor-intensive details of day-to-day life at a time when the common folk knew no such thing as retirement.

July 2, 1912   Dunbarton, Wisconsin

Dear son

your letter of the 7-1 rec'd yesturday   I will Send you in this letter $200 I have Some money in the Bank that is subject to check & not drawing interest & you might as well use it as to let it lay there

the wool is about all in   Terry & I could not make a deal So he started home on this morning train   We had a great rain Sunday morning and a terrible rain at about 4 o clock in the after noon with a high wind   Some of our Peas are pretty old to use now   currents all Pick & Part of the Goos Berryes   O that rain was fine

we are all about the same   no nues

with love I will close   I am sleepy this 20 min past 10 AM

your father F B

later

your ma washed yesturday and now is a going to squeze juise out of currents for Jell   I have bin to the store with 2 1/2 D **(dozen)** *Eggs   that is about what your ma gets a day   I am going to send mas rose* **(a rose mother grew)** *in this for Addie* **(the pressed rose was still between the pages of the letter when discovered in 1997)**

Oh Addie the Owls have come back   do you remember the one that came so near us while we were out in my Bower **(flower garden)**   *remmber the vines that reachd the top of that apple tree north of the seat this year they are growing to mak a record*

I may not see you before you go to to n.y.   I hope you will have a good time out their   and the children will ceep well

PS I may come down to see your ma hide while you are both gone & wee would have a time wouldent wee   do you think she would go to church with me

Loudon was not satisfied with running a wallpaper store. He was always casting about for something which would provide a better income. In 1913 he almost fell prey to one of the land scams which plagued the country from the wilds of Alaska to the swamps of Florida.

This letter is to acknowledge receipt of Loudon's $10 down-payment for a lot in Willow River, British Columbia, Canada. Enclosed with the letter is an invoice for the balance of $240 and a contract to be signed and returned.

A flyer with the letter indicates the location of Willow River. The flyer states that with two proposed railroads crossing each other on the banks of a navigable stream, people who buy lots in 1913 will be able to sell them and double their money the next year. There is also a copy of the Willow River newspaper (Vol. 1, No. 1), and every article boasts excitement over the coming railways and touts property

values.   Neither railroad was ever built, and the town never materialized. At this writing it is still one of the most inaccessible and remote places in North America.

Loudon has gotten cold feet over the Canadian tundra (so to speak) and has wisely refrained from sending any more money to the schemers.

The letter is a prime example of the overly formal style of business writing then in vogue.

May 19, 1913   Willow River, Canada

Mr. Loudon Blackbourn,

Dear Sir:-

We beg to acknowledge receipt of your esteemed favor of the 14th with $10 enclosed, being first payment on lot 7 of block 57, district lot 782, for which please find herewith enclosed reservation receipt #4.

We have been asked so many times - "WHERE IS WILLOW RIVER?" To settle doubts as to this matter once and for all time, it is a subdivision of Lot 788, Group 1, Cariboo District, British Columbia, Canada.

It is currently reported that Willow River is to be a divisional point of the Grand Trunk Pacific railway.   The company makes no official confirmation of this fact, but we will be much more surprised if it were not true, than if it were.

Navigation to Willow River will soon be open and hundreds of people will be going in. Now is the time to buy, before prices are advanced, and before the first of the railroads arrives, as by that time prices will probably have more than doubled, and all the choice locations will have been taken.

Promptly send the balance due on your lot. Then make the decision to purchase another, do not put it off. Do it to-day. There are only a few

Joyce and Rosamond Blackbourne ready for winter weather, 1914.

tracts left. Fill out the application blank enclosed, and return it to us with down payment by return mail.

Trusting to hear from you by return mail and again thanking you for your application, we beg to remain,

Yours very truly,

Pacific Land & Townsites Co. Ltd.

Loudon has given up the idea of being a storekeeper in Brodhead. He has given up on his brief temptation to try to make money as a land speculator. What he *has* decided to do is go into farming--in New York state of all places. He has scraped together enough for a down payment and intends to buy the farm on land contract.

Loudon is interested in buying a farm owned by a Mr. Woodman. Following is a high-pressure sales letter from the realtor, and the tactics seem to be pretty much the same as in use by some business people eighty-odd years later.

January 7, 1915   Wood, Parker & Blair, Morrisville, New York

Mr. L Blackbourne,

Dear Sir:-

We have before us your letter of December 20th. You will remember that you requested us once before to go after Woodman and try and get him down **(get the price down)**. *We succeeded in getting off $200. We know positively that the price is now the very least that will buy the farm.*

The writer has been acquainted with that farm for over forty years. I rented it for a term of three years and know it to be a good farm if properly handled. The place is pleasantly situated only two miles from town. The land lays positively and the pasture is watered with never failing springs.

167

One farm of 192 acres recently listed at $2,850; another of 108 acres at $4,600. We of course had as soon sell one place as the other, but we believe that you, Mr. Blackbourne, are making a great mistake in not closing for the Woodman property before someone else gets it. We have had many people here and have sold two properties nearby but have refrained from showing this property, believing that you appreciated the fact that it was well worth the money.

Mr. Harp, whose place you saw near Pratts Hollow, and whom said he would reduce his price $500 for you came in this week and told us to put the $500 back on the first price. Values are certainly increasing.

We have a man from So. Dakota here looking for a farm like the Woodman property, however, we are going to refrain from showing him this farm until we hear from you.

Awaiting your reply, we beg to remain

Yours very truly

Wood, Parker and Blair Agts.

Loudon, of course, concludes that the Woodman farm is a pretty good deal for the price. He borrows the down-payment of $800 from brother Fred and buys the place with a mortgage owed to Mr. Woodman in the amount of $1650. Loudon receives a deed in the mail, which mundane document is not repeated here, and he receives an itemized list of what he is getting for $2,450--which fascinating document *is* presented on the following page.

The *bobbs* which are listed are detachable sled runners for hauling logs.

168

Property Woodman Farm

142 acres, house, barn, buildings	*$699.00*
1 pair horses	*150*
12 cows	*840*
4 calves	*65*
100 hens	*75*
3 wagons	*65*
2 harness	*20*
harrow	*10*
1500 ft logs	*18*
1 sled	*5*
all small tools	*10*
1 Pr bobbs	*10*
milk cans	*5*
1 mower	*20*
rake	*5*
Hay rack	*5*
Plows	*5*
Cultivator	*3*
1 fat hog	*25*
Hay, Estimated 35 tons	*400*
2 Heating stoves	*15*
	————
	$2,450.00

In the early spring of 1915 Loudon takes wife Addie, daughters Rosamond and Joyce, and their grandma Hannah to a farm near Morrisville, New York. His intention is to stay with it for a growing season to determine whether it will pay. It doesn't. By late fall the family is back in the home in Brodhead, and Loudon is trying to sell the New York farm.

Loudon's new vocation is to sell brushes door-to-door throughout southwestern Wisconsin. Addie writes letters to him for personal pickup (general delivery) at Post Offices on Loudon's itinerary. She refers to Woodman, the person who holds the land contract. And, she uses an unusual phrase, "scratch up," meaning "hurry up."

It is probably on Addie's mind that she is repeating her mother's lifestyle as she writes to her husband during his extended sales trips. She has hired a teenage girl to help with house work while she and her children are sick.

March 22, 1916 Brodhead, Wisconsin

Dear Loudon:-

Well Woodman's letter showed up last night. I rather believe that neither Kimball nor anyone else is going to buy that farm. So I think you had better scratch up **(hurry up)** *and get the thing settled with Woodman. I think Woodman would like to move back there or he can get a renter all right.*

Joyce is up around the house but her cough still sounds the same. Dr. Mitchell put both her and Rosamond on a tonic Monday. I wish he hadnt been quite so pig-headed when I wanted him to do something for Joyce two weeks ago. Her coughs worry me. Rosamond looks awfully pale and thin.

The night before was a terrible night--thunder and lightning, rain, sleet, and in the morning there was six inches of snow. Of course this hired girl won't shovel snow. And I supposed our regular shoveler would come but he never showed up. In the afternoon I phoned for Wells and he got here and got it cleaned.

Ma seems to feel better this morning and yesterday sat up quite a lot. She walks stronger but I am afraid she will tumble over. Mrs. Stewart died yesterday, so her troubles are over.

Celia came Tuesday morning. She helps out some. She wants $4.50 per week if she also washes laundry. I hate to pay so much for help. I let her make a chocolate pudding yesterday, and it took her an hour and a half. There is coal yet, but I ordered half a ton. I've been so dizzy I've had to hang on to things when I walk. I hope we'll get out of the woods some time.

Dear me. I do miss you so. Well, good bye with love from all,

Addie

This letter is unusual, for it is a letter from Loudon to Mr. Woodman. It is part of the collection because Loudon retained a handwritten copy. The letter reveals that Loudon has not hit his stride yet, financially. He is 37 and must wait another year to find himself in a career.

March 27, 1916   Brodhead, Wisconsin

Mr. William Woodman

Dear Sir:

Thanking you for agreeing to buy the farm from me for $1 and the mortgage. I havent made any payments or the interest as I havent been able to raise the money to do so, but I have managed to pay the taxes.

Taking the farm back for the mortgage you will make a good thing out of it. I borrowed the money for the down payment which you received and I still must pay back that loan, so I am the loser.

Sincerely,

Loudon Blackbourne

Loudon is working as a traveling salesman for the North Ridge Brush Company of Freeport, Illinois. This activity will last about a year. To be a salesman in 1916 one would take a train to a village, secure a room at a hotel, and head out on foot with a sample case to make house-to-house calls.

The head of the brush company, Henry Northridge, was fond of writing motivational letters to his sales staff. He sent a letter to his sales representatives nearly every week, and specially printed letterhead for these occasions was titled, "Monday Morning Visits."

Here's an interesting example of Henry's cheerleader personality.

December 2, 1916   Freeport, Illinois

Dear Mr. Blackbourn:

I'm writing you in this personal way asking your co-operation to the limit.

In the tremendous undertaking of breaking all previous records in a single week's business.

The week set for this gigantic undertaking is between Monday morning, December 4th and Saturday evening, December 9th.

I think -- I believe -- I know that it can be done. But it's going to take red-blooded men and women to do it.

Won't you drop me a line telling me that I can count on you for the best you've got next week.

Cordially,

J. Henry Northridge

Afterthought -- There is a prize to the first man or woman selling $100 worth of brushes -- cop it for yourself.

Loudon writes to his six-year-old daughter. He is at Cassville, Wisconsin and is going to ride a ferry boat across the Mississippi River to make sales calls at Turkey River, Iowa.

December 12, 1916   Cassville, Wisconsin

Dear little Joyce

Glad to get your letter. I expect to have a ride on the river to go to a town called Turkey River. I am not anxious about it, either. The river has a smell I don't like.

They say the river is 600 feet across here and 26 feet deep. It is most 8 oclock and I must get busy.

With hugs and kisses

Papa

This is Fred Blackbourne's last letter to Loudon. Fred is 87, and a testament to the American Dream. He came here at age ten, penniless and without parents or education. He expected the American government to defend the shores, deliver the mail, and stay out of his life--and that's basically what it did for him. With neither help nor meddling from society, Fred created a meaningful life for himself and his children.

Fred left his estate in trust to his children with his wife, Victoria, having life use of it. When she died in 1932 at age 92, there was still over $20,000 remaining--a major amount of money in an era of $600-a-year incomes.

Fred was a fair employer, a major benefactor of the church, and a leader in the Masonic Lodge. The enclosure mentioned in Fred's letter was still in the letter when it was opened by the author in 1997--a five dollar gold piece dated 1893.

January 5, 1917   Dunbarton, Wisconsin

Dear son and daughter

*it has bin snowing here to day   i see some horses that have bin pulling
hard and there is steam rising off there backs   i am having trouble geting
around to do the chores   i walk just a short ways and i get short of
breath*

*i am inclosing some thing for you   say hello to Addie rosamon and joyce
i will write more when i am not so tired*

your Father Fred

At the beginning of 1917 Loudon Blackbourne has secured a position
in the Woodford State Bank. Banking is to prove to be his only love
in the world of work. While Loudon has never succeeded in making
a fortune firsthand, he is quite adept at making money with money.
He proves to be good at banking and he is a natural with both
financial matters and the public. He rents a room upstairs in the
fairly new, attractive brick bank building and commutes the thirty-
some miles to home in Brodhead on weekends.

At first Loudon commutes via railroad. It's a convenient route with
a change of trains at Dill.   But, in 1920 he will buy his first
automobile--a Model T Ford, of course; and help to ensure the
lengthy but thorough demise of the American rural passenger train.
The tracks will be ripped out of Woodford in 1942.

This letter is from brother, Fred. The era is the tail end of American
rugged individualism and self-sufficiency. Fred lives in Dunbarton,
a short distance from his father's cheese factory. He runs the only
store in town, and his family raises most of their own food.
Astonishingly, Fred has saved nearly every penny he has earned the
previous year.

Fred's letterhead is fascinating. While the year is 1917, the graphics
are right out of the previous century.

February 12, 1917   Dunbarton, Wisconsin

Dear Bro.

I heard as how you were located at Woodford. I understand the merchant there wished to sell out and move to Texas. Say I would like to move South providing I could find a decent climate minus chiggars and fleas.

As a banker you had ought to know everything about business. Do you think stores at Woodford are making good? I made over $1800 last year. My interest money rec'd was $462.74 so you see the store netted me a little better than $1400. Out of all I saved a little over $1800. Well we have to spend <u>some</u> money in a year. I would like to save $5000 a year for 5 yrs then take it easy.

I weigh 172   lost 4 lb

Any news? give me history of Woodford. Ever see Hank? Will come over to see you in fishing season

yours

Fred

Only a day later, Fred writes to Loudon again. This time the topic is their father's estate. German-Americans and the German language have come to be called "Dutch" because of anti-German sentiment at the time of World War I (1914-1918).

February 13, 1917   Dunbarton, Wisconsin

Dear Bro

Our letters must have crossed   I don't know about the division of father's estate.   The chances are it may be only a partial distribution.   A considerable sum of mortgages are not due father yet, and you know banks wont buy mortgages at 5-5 1/2 %   they would want them discounted.

Sell the old creamery for 1000 or $1200 if you can   I have half a notion to advertise in the Swiss or Dutch paper of Monroe but don't know the cheese paper address.   You see if I can sell the old separators it would make me happy.   if I could get $100 or $150 each it would help some.   did I tell you Fathers tax would be over $600.

Say I went out tonight about 7 or 7-15 and shot a duck   probably 3 or 4 but found only one.

Brother Fred

This letter from Loudon's brother, Fred, completes our visit to the turn of the twentieth century. Loudon has paid off the last of a loan from Fred, and Fred is returning the note to him. Then Fred launches into an interesting monologue about their brother, Jesse. The details reveal much about the conditions of life at the time. Being a Christian of the times, Fred doesn't spell out the word *devil*, but abbreviates it.

March 10, 1917   Dunbarton, Wisconsin

Dear Bro.

Here is your note.   many thanks

Now I was up to Shullsburg   Jamison is to let me know last of next week if he can find some money for Jess @ 5%   Gosh Jess is a hard proposition   his horses are so poor & weak dont see how he will ever get any farming done   Same every Spring everything too poor to skin   last year he had no crop   bought horses as colts now they are crowbaits so how can he do anything

I wrote him that he could make more to sell farm and loan money to somebody else as mortgage & do nothing   he would have 8 or $900 a year. this way I dont think he can make $200 a year farming and save it he never has   You cant do nothing with him   I dont go there he dont come here. there is no help for Jess   he is worse off than old Ben Wiley or Pete McDonald   he has notes neighbors have signed he don't pay the interest   he would never pay any principle I wrote him about it.

*he and his wife are not capable of making a living   she wont let him pay his debts and she would rather starve the cattle & horses than buy feed I never seen things go so badly   if our mother bot **(bought)** a team for him every Spring he would starve them in winter and what can you do? Jess told me 10 months since that Ella is to handle all the money. I told him to handle his own money pay his own bills if he couldn't do that I would have a guardian appointed   told him that last year, and he never came over since*

the poor goose is solely represented by Ella   there is no Jess   there never will be   Jess died 20 years ago   he is worse than a baby in her hands   now the poor fool is after other women   oh say its awful to see one go to the d---l like Jess has. its worse than death   I spose they will try to get all of mothers money

well I am glad Mrs. Hyde is recovering

177

Is there any money being made in Woodford stores   You see the way
people do here they lag behind on their charge accounts with me just
enough so we can't put money out on interest   so we lose out on money
that should be ours just because people don't pay their bills on time hard
to make a living here   Dunbarton is a catalog town   possibly Sears &
Roebuck & Co would buy fathers factory and land

Well give me all the news

Yours as ever

Fred

The turn of the twentieth century was a wonderful era in American
history. The nation came of age as a world power. Dramatic advances in
technology altered the face of American civilization from one of horse
power, wood, and steam to one of horsepower, steel, and oil. The United
States had entered the new century with boundless energy and soaring
optimism, and that process was mirrored in a minor sort of way in the
transformation of the Smith family into the Blackbourne family.

CHAPTER SEVEN

THE ROARING TWENTIES AND DEPRESSED THIRTIES, 1920-1939

We are now well into the twentieth century. All the pioneer generation with whom we started are gone, except for Victoria Blackbourne who will live well into her nineties and Hannah Maria Allen Smith Hyde who will pass away in 1921.

Let's recall Hannah for a moment. She was the beloved mother and grandmother of the Blackbournes. She remembered President Jackson, and had heard Jenny Lind--the Swedish Nightingale--sing. She had bought a souvenir at the World's Fair in 1853 and saw the Crystal Palace's hall of art with its 1200 gas lights. She had come to the treeless, burr-infested prairie and lost three out of four children and two husbands and kept her faith. She had done hard labor to keep from losing her home. She had lived to see the United States become the leading world power; and had lived to see hundred-mile-per-hour trains, electric lights, telephones, automobiles, and airplanes. Her 83 years had comprised quite a life.

This chapter begins with Rosamond and Joyce as children, and it ends with them as school teachers. Loudon and Addie deal with mid-life crises and pass their prime in this chapter. And as ever, the world continues its eternal process of change.

Joyce and Rosamond Blackbourne.

180

Addie's first-cousin, Grace, writes to Rosamond and Joyce. The girls are 10 and 11 years old, and Grace writes the perfect letter for children. This letter is all we know of Grace, but it is enough to prompt the conclusion that she was a bright and sensitive lady, and educated.

April 25, 1920   Hoosick Falls, New York

Dear Rosamond & Joyce:-

Just a short letter to let my girlies know I am thinking of them. This is Sunday afternoon and as we are not having any Service today I am writing a letter or two.

It is bright today but there is such a cold wind that it is more comfortable in the house.

I am enclosing some verses which I think you will like. I like them all. I like the Dutch Lullaby; I love to think of those little Dutch babies going to sleep and "the windmills go whirling around." The little picture reminds me of when I was a little girl and my Grandma cut out just such paper dolls for me. Your Grandma Hyde has made lots of such dolls I think.

We are having a late spring. It will seem good to have warm weather. Last Tuesday was lovely and I sat on the back porch in the sunshine, and while sitting there I saw a mouse asleep in the sunshine. I did feel a little like Miss Muffett whom the spider frightened away, however. I stayed and found Miss Mouse would not stir unless you touched her two or three times. Fortunate for Miss Mouse that my cats Prince and Teddy did not come along.

And, while I was on the porch Mr. & Mrs. Chickadee came and made a great fuss because I was there. They wanted to build a nest just about my head. You see I had quite a time trying to enjoy the sunshine on the porch. I try to keep out of doors all I can. I am feeling better than awhile ago, but still far from well. Aunt Ette & Eloise are well as usual.

181

Do you like dandelions? I do. We have had several crops of them already this spring.

Love & a kiss to your mother and aunt Rie. Much love & kisses to you both. And I am

Lovingly yours,

Cousin Grace

One of the first trips which the Blackbourne family takes in an automobile is to Wisconsin Dells. It is 1922 and the automobile is Loudon's first--a Model T Ford. Today the uneventful trip takes less than two hours. But read about the ordeal which is involved in taking a Model T over 90 miles of gravel and sand roads.

A *dell* is a steep river valley. Since the 1860s the dells of the Wisconsin River have increased in popularity as a tourist attraction. At the time Rosamond writes, the village where the boat trips begin is named "Kilbourn." Later the village will change its name to, "Wisconsin Dells," a city whose "strip" will offer miles of roadside entertainments. But in 1922 it is a sleepy village nestled amidst a vast jackpine forest, and the only attraction is the scenic waterway.

Of note is the fact that Rosamond is writing a description of her trip at age 13, the age of her mother when she wrote of her visit to the Statue of Liberty.

Our Trip to the Dells

July 20, 1922

We packed our car with luggage tied on the running boards and left home at 6 am. On the way to Madison we had a tire blow out and papa had to put on the spare. Three hours later we got to Madison. We found the canvas and awning dealer and rented a tent. Then we proceeded toward Baraboo.

South of Baraboo is an awful large hill. Our car stalled because the gas wouldn't flow to the motor. This was happening to many other cars. Papa and some men pushed the car around so it faced backward. Then the motor would run and we could go up the hill in reverse. Only the sand was too deep and we got stuck. Papa got out gunny sacks and twine and tied the sacks around the tires so we wouldn't sink in the sand so bad. Next the motor over heated. Papa took a bucket to the creek which flows along the road and had to wait a long while for the radiator to cool off before he dared to put the cold water in.

Before we got to the top another tire went flat. Papa didn't have another spare. He put another inner tube in the flat tire and pumped it up by hand. It made him awfully tired.

When we got within sight of Baraboo we stopped at a farm to ask if we could camp in their cow pasture. It didn't rain, for a good thing. The next day we drove on to Kilbourn. We had another flat tire on the way. In the afternoon we rode the boat on the river. The cliffs were awful pretty but I was mighty glad to get back on solid ground as none of our family can swim.

We camped that night with a good many other travelers in the village park. The next day we pulled out for home.

Rosamond Blackbourne

By 1923 Loudon Blackbourne has moved from the bank in the small village of Woodford to the bank in the larger village of Argyle. He receives a letter from the president of the Woodford bank asking him to come back. Loudon stands by his decision and remains with the bank at Argyle. He doesn't know how fickle fate intends to be--six years later the Argyle bank is destined to fail following the crash of the stock market; seventy-five years later (as this is being written) the Woodford State Bank is still a going concern with a new building and branch offices.

The bank president uses a turn of words for which time has altered the meaning. Today the phrase, "if you have any desire to go on in

this world," would probably be taken to mean, "if you want to live!" In 1923 it meant, "if you want to get ahead."

March 24, 1923   Woodford, Wisconsin

Dear Friend Loudon

The Directors here seem quite unanimous in wanting your assistance as Cashier. If you have any desire to go on in this world, I believe you will do well to give this your favorable consideration.

You have the privilege to come back here now and thru May 1st. What services I can give in aiding you will be gladly given.

I trust you will consider it.

Yours Very Truly,

M. H. Olson, President

Rosamond is spending a week with her father in Argyle during the summer and writes to her mother and sister at home. She is 14 and displays some of the timeless attitudes of youth.

July 14, 1923   Argyle, Wisconsin

Dear Mama and Joyce,

I'm down at the "pank"--at least that's what the Swiss call it--with Papa. I have been helping sort checks and I typed some letters for him. That took a long time as you know I don't know how to type. The place has been closed for business for a long time, but Papa seems to keep finding things to do. It is now four minutes and fourteen seconds past 5 o'clock P. M., Central Standard Time. Papa told me to be patient and we will get ice cream for dessert when we have supper.

184

I think Argyle is the hottest place in the Central Standard Time zone. Papa says after supper we can drive up to Wiota to cool off because it is on top of a hill and there is usually a breeze.

From your baked Rosamond

PS: At least I am not "half baked."

This letter is written in the summer between Rosamond's graduation from high school and her start of college at the University of Wisconsin in Madison. Four years later she will have graduated with high honors. At this writing her experience-base still sounds quite childlike, but the letter reveals her intelligence and upward-bound spirit. The letter begins in Latin ("my friend Joyce") and ends in French. In comparing the mechanics of this letter with letters from earlier generations, one can conclude that education does make a difference.

The letter is written from Argyle where Rosamond and Addie are staying with Loudon. Joyce is visiting a friend in Monroe. The letter talks about returning to Brodhead after taking Joyce to Monroe, then departing the next day for Argyle.

July 28, 1927   Argyle, Wisconsin

Mea Joyce Cara,

How are you? I am fine except that I am pretty "darn" hot. I am sweating great big spikes. It is now 10:23 Central Standard Time. I have just got through cutting out my new pajamas. I will have to go to town to get some more thread **(people who lived in towns commonly called a shopping trip, "going to town").** *Mama is fixing the beans.*

I got up at five o'clock yesterday and picked all the "ratches," **(radishes)** *papa picked the berries--two qts, anyway--and mama weeded and picked some flowers. We left Brodhead about seven and got here about nine* **(two hours to go 28 miles in the Model T)** *and packed in all our junk. I was* *tired by nightfall and the bed laid "awful good." I laid "plunk" in the middle and kicked around all I wanted to. But believe you me it was hot. There was a nice breeze from the south that blew the curtain all the way to the bed so I didn't suffer so bad.*

Mama sure was "snorry." She gave such a snort that it woke me up and I "rized up" right out of bed. It took me a minute to figure out what on Earth it was. Well this has been quite a paragraph--I didn't study Hinglish fer nothin! When you see the subject of the next paragraph, you will see that my transitions aren't very good, either.

Mama says that I am qualified to be inducted into the "Order of the Black Hand," for I have not yet learned the gentile art of washing dishes as she does. Me, I figure you can save a lot of time and water if you just wipe 'em! Ha Ha Ho Ho

At last your poor "over-kitchened" sister bids "Au Revoir."

Rosamond

About 1920 a new Methodist minister came to Brodhead. His name was Waters, and he and Loudon became the best of friends. Loudon was only home on weekends and spent much time in the company of Waters. Addie confided to her daughters that she was jealous of the time which Waters had with her husband. By the end of Addie's life Loudon was a devoted and adoring husband. Perhaps there was a time in the middle of their marriage when his interest waned. Addie did, after all, age rapidly. At 50, Loudon looked 50; at 50, Addie looked 75. Perhaps an identity crisis at mid-life is not something unique to the present generation.

This letter is from Tom Waters to Loudon after Waters has left Brodhead to serve a new congregation. Does he seem just ever so slightly cynical for a man of God? He reveals both the light and the dark side of human nature all in the same letter--it's unusual.

186

August 14, 1927   New Richmond, Wisconsin

Dear Loudon:

It is a pleasure to be able to write to you this morning. I am pleased to say that I find high interest among my new congregation. The young people are especially interested in church matters, and as I gaze out at my full house from the pulpit on Sunday mornings I am pleased to see that their average age must be 16.

The singing here lacks the artistic touches of that at Brodhead, but it is really fine congregational singing. I am sad to say that division and dissension are already rife here. I don't know how long I will be willing to play lackey for this bunch of Norwegians and Swedes. They go out on Saturday nights and drink their damn rotgut bootleg booze and then come to church Sunday and pretend to be pious. I look at them and hate their guts and smile and pretend to be their benevolent father figure.

This is not to say that they are any worse than the factions in Brodhead. They never seemed able to keep their filthy claws off me. Please let me assure you upon oath that I did not see Marjorie again. My wife is all worked up about it and, of course, you may imagine just what sort of thing that is to have rankling on the mind and in the heart of our home. I am sorry this is bruited about; but hope you will tell my friends that it is not true. I suppose the saints there have done this in order to turn even my friends against me. I believe the interests of the Kingdom of God would be well served if that church were closed up.

I am grateful that I am a minister, and that I can work out my own salvation contemporaneously with that of trying to win other's. Write often, I look for it and need your prayers.

Tom

This letter is written from Argyle where Addie is spending a week with Loudon. Usually he stays in Argyle alone, returning home to Brodhead on weekends. It is written to Rosamond who is a Freshman

in college and to Joyce who is spending a few days visiting Rosamond. Addie always referred to her daughters as "little." Her identity was so centered in motherhood that she never wanted to accept their growing up. Later, her daughter Joyce practiced motherhood the same way. "Reading between the lines," one can sense Loudon's distance from Addie and her despair over it. At age 48 Loudon was realizing that his youthful dreams of great financial success weren't going to materialize, and that he and his wife were passing the prime of their physical appearance--new burdens to which he did not readily adapt.

November 3, 1927   Argyle, Wisconsin

Dear little Joyce and Rosamond:-

Well did you have a fire drill last night?   There wasn't any here.   We arrived about twenty to ten last night.   Our trip was without accident or getting lost.

This morning your father arose about seven and so did I.   He hustled off, but had to come back after his glasses, so I was ready by that time and walked down town with him.   I went in to Blaisdell's and got my breakfast, and he went on to the bank!   I ate 3 slices of toast fried egg and coffee for 20 cents.

I saw Mr. Berget through the store window so I stopped in a minute to speak to him.   I walked clear around the business section.   It acted like a storm but seems to be clearing off some.   I am kind of up a stump to know what to do next.   I wonder if you slept good.   I slept pretty good.   I guess I won't call on anyone before dinner.   I really don't know where to go first. The trees are all bare.

Hope you like the ball game.   Will you wear light dresses to the banquet? Do as you like there.   I am going to do as I please here and take it easy. I will have to eat dinner alone too I suppose.   The house is as still as a tomb.

Well, I guess there is no news I know of. Good bye--with heaps of love and kisses from your

Mother

Addie has gone to Madison to spend a weekend with Rosamond at Chadbourne Hall to attend the annual tea given for the girls' mothers. She took a bus to Madison on Friday afternoon, but Loudon and Joyce will drive to retrieve her on Sunday. In the brief interval of her absence from home, she writes a short note to Joyce.

The first settlers in southern Wisconsin were New Englanders of English ancestry--Addie's parents among them. The great influx of later immigrants were Swiss, German, and Norwegian. Addie has heard their conversation so much that this English woman lapses into German syntax, "I will look for you a dress."

May 17, 1928   Chadbourne Hall, University of Wisconsin

Dear Little Joyce:-

I arrived here safe and sound. The bus was late in Janesville so we didn't leave till five o'clock. It wasn't loaded so heavy and it bobbed around a good deal and my head aches now so I guess when we mail this I'll get some aspirin.

It was six:thirty when I got to the Madison bus station. I decided to mosey up here, but after a block I decided to ride the street car and rode right up to the corner here.

I found Rosamond and talked with some of her friends. Then we got something to eat and went over to the band concert up in front of Bascom Hall.

When you come to get me on Sunday make your father leave plenty early. While I am here I will look for you a dress. Then I suppose you won't like it.

Well, good-night dearie. Mother

This letter comes to Rosamond a few days prior to her graduation from college. It is 1931 and the Great Depression is in full swing. Most school districts have effected a hiring freeze. Only three members of Rosamond's College of Education graduating class are destined to find teaching jobs, and hiring is being done strictly on the basis of grade-point average. Rosamond has the second-highest GPA in her class, and thus is one of the three people to be hired.

Rosamond's teaching job is in Antigo, a mill town in northern Wisconsin. While living there, she will travel the few miles to see the ravaged "road house" called "Little Bohemia," where the fledgling FBI has had a colossal shoot-out with the Dillinger gang (Dillinger got away). The mayhem prompted Will Rogers to quip: "The only way the FBI will ever shoot Dillinger is if he happens to be standing too close to some innocent bystanders!"

Rosamond's starting annual salary as an honor graduate of the University of Wisconsin is $700. The next year--1932--with the Depression worsening, her salary is reduced to $600. When Rosamond posed the question, "How do you expect a single woman to live on $600 a year?" the reply came, "You can go live with your parents in the summer."

At the time, incidentally, a new Model A Ford cost $600. Sixty-five years later, a teacher's starting salary is still just about the price of a new Ford. Inflation has drastically altered the numbers, but some relative values have remained the same.

June 19, 1931   The University of Wisconsin, Madison

Dear Miss Blackbourne:

I deem it a privilege, on behalf of the Dean of your college, to inform you that the Faculty voted this morning to grant you senior honors. Although it is not the custom of the University to place any designation of honors on the diploma, I want you to know that it is proper for you to regard yourself as being awarded the baccalaureate degree "cum laude." You will

190

Rosamond Blackbourne, a college graduate in 1932.

Victoria Blackbourne, age 92.

receive a fourragere, a gold cord to be worn from the left shoulder of the academic gown at Commencement.

Yours very sincerely,

Charles A. Smith
Secretary of the Faculty

Now it is 1933 and Victoria Blackbourne has died at the age of 93. Fred Blackbourne, Junior is the executor for the estate. He writes to Loudon regarding the estate's final accounting. Loudon had promised to send his daughters to college, and their college years spanned 1927-1933. The Great Depression began in 1929 and the Argyle bank closed. Loudon then returned permanently to Brodhead where he opened a gas station. The money for the gas station and his daughters' schooling was borrowed from his mother. Throughout their lives, Rosamond and Joyce never knew that their father had to borrow money to keep them at the university.

By now Fred has given up trying to operate a general store in Dunbarton (though others operated the business into the 1960's). He has moved the few miles to Shullsburg where he is operating a farm implement business (still operated by his descendants at this writing).

The amount of the estate may seem trivial by current standards. But, in 1933 Rosamond was teaching school for $600 a year. Based upon that standard, Victoria's estate was equivalent to 32 years' income.

April 12, 1933   Shullsburg, Wisconsin

Dear brother Loudon:-

Enclosed you will find your copy of the final accounting of mothers estate.

Joyce Blackbourne as a college graduate in 1933.

The total assets remaining amount to a gross of $19,453.77. You took notes from mother in 1930, 1931, and 1932 and from me in 1930. The unpaid balance of these notes is $1,197.25. There are five heirs at $2,953.48 each. Deducting balance on notes you are due $289.13 from mothers estate.

Your brother   Fred

It is 1934 and Rosamond is about to celebrate her twenty-fifth birthday. Any mid-life distance which Addie and Loudon might have felt a few years earlier has been healed by the perseverance of their relationship. Loudon's note reveals that Rosamond's parents are back "on track" as a loving couple.

February 4, 1934   Brodhead, Wisconsin

Dear Little Rosamond:

Happy birthday to you. I remember what a cute little blue eyed youngster you were and always have been. Your ma and I went around shopping for a gift until she found something that suited her. I too thought it pretty. She did it up real cute to send. She also made a cake but said she couldn't send it with frosting. I told her to make the frosting anyway and we'd keep it. I had some after supper and it was good.

My cold is convalescent but not quite vanished. It is still quite conspicuous, especially the red trimming 'round the nose.

According to Joyce, her calendar is quite full the rest of her school year with play practice etc. Time passes quickly when one is busy.

I am expecting a load of gas. The Cities Service are putting out a new Ethyl, so that should make more pep in their gasoline. There was lots of trade yesterday and last night.

This Monday morning it is snowing large flakes so probably it wont last long. The ground is white and getting whiter and it is not cold.

There is nothing new so I am signing off with much love and adoration to little blue eyes.

Papa

This letter concludes our visit to the twenties and thirties. Of note in this letter is mention of a young pianist which Rosamond and Addie have heard in the dining room of a Milwaukee hotel. Rosamond has known him as West Milwaukee High School student, Wladziu (Walter) Valentino Liberace. One day he will begin billing his performances by merely his last name, and that name will become famous the world over.

March 1, 1939

Dear Little Rosamond:-

Have you been listening to Eddie cantor. He has been pretty good tonight. I guess I'll shut off the radio so I can write. I tried to write while he was talking and got in a great mess.

We had a wonderful visit to Milwaukee didn't we. It was so nice of the young man to play The Beautiful Blue Danube for me when we had dinner at the Plankinton. I had never heard it played so well.

I'm not well today and I feel rather lonesome. It was about ten when I was able to get up. I must quit for I have to write a line to Joyce. Lots of love and kisses for you

Mother

The Brodhead home in the 1930s.

The decade of the twenties saw America attain a pinnacle of peace, prosperity, and well-being the like of which it had never known before. In a sense, the nation had come fully into the beginnings of a healthy and robust middle age. This condition mirrored perfectly the status of Addie and Loudon Blackbourne in their personal lives.

With the coming of the Great Depression in the decade of the thirties, a great deal of the luster tarnished from the splendid Ship of State. Addie and Loudon, too, mirrored a personal depression in the passing of their prime of life and in the financial disappointments which they endured.

By strenuous effort nations can regain their youthful vigor, as the United States did following the Depression and World War II. Families can revitalize from one generation to the next, too. The stage was set for the baton of healthy maturity to be passed from the Blackbournes to their children.

196

CHAPTER EIGHT

THE ROMANTIC FORTIES, 1939-1945

The decade of the forties--indeed, the first *half* of the forties--brings about tremendous change. The world order and the technology of day-to-day existence are altered almost overnight. On the personal level, Rosamond and Joyce leave their younger years behind them and begin serious romantic relationships. Addie and Loudon enter an era which undeniably must be considered old age.

The first two letters in this chapter are from late in 1939. They are included here because they are really part of the story of the forties.

Now it is 1939. Rosamond has now moved from Antigo to Oconomowoc, a desirable far-western Milwaukee suburb. The previous summer she attended summer school at Columbia University in New York City where, several summers hence she will receive a master's degree. While in New York she has met and briefly dated one Reginald Rogers.

Now, Reginald is quite the urbane character. The next several letters shall treat the reader to his ultra-sophisticated prose. At first blush he would appear to be the perfect match for Rosamond's intellect and refinement. This first letter does everything to establish that conclusion. But the reader will be intrigued with Reginald's future letters where his hidden agenda comes ever more clearly into focus. Fortunately for Rosamond, she has been cautious and questioning from the start.

These letters from Reginald are presented together here as block, and without further introductory commentary. *Do* enjoy the drama--and, oh, doesn't he present an interesting study in style!

August 13, 1939   New York City, New York

Dear Rosamond

New York City this evening doesn't have that setting which one week ago this hour I found so truly delightful.

How does it seem to be back again--away from the heat, the books, and the unaccustomed late hours? To be ensconced among friends is a factor --a big factor--that contributes much to the happiness accruing from a trip. I think one will not gainsay there is any place quite like home.

As a boy, and I am pretty much of a one now, a homecoming to me presented moments of unforgettable joy. Where else can one find people so dear, so appreciative of your and of my very being? I, too, have frequently found the rest of the world somewhat callous in this regard. This afternoon, along toward three o'clock, I will say, I had occasion to bolt through Grand Central Station----you know, where we one grand

198

evening walked on one level and then another. My consciousness turned to the lines of passengers then boarding today's "Commodore Vanderbilt."

How unthoughtful of me in my having detained you Saturday from obtaining a better seat! I did remain, unseen by you, until the last lights of your train had flickered off into the distance, leaving New York somehow not quite the same for me ever again.

To answer questions you posed, but to which I never replied:

Yes, I'll wade through sand with you. Any time.

Yes, I'll let you stuff fried chicken into my suit pockets when you think me too formal.

No, I do not merely try to say "pretty things." I am not one practiced in platitudes. They are not my soul's beatitudes. Expressions coming from me are sincere. My every moment with you is a treasured memory.

I want you to know that I never had a better time in Rainbow Grill with anyone than you.

Sincerely,

Reginald

October 9, 1939   New York City, New York

Dear Rosamond

You are a grand letter writer. I wish to convey an impression of the delight that comes to me with the arrival of your letters.

If I were in Oconomowoc I would walk with you around that Lake. I am fond of walking as you know, and walking with you lends much to such an enjoyment.

A week so highlighted by hours of overtime has rendered me somewhat weary. I wouldn't want any pictures of myself as you saw me this summer. Fatigue from late hours was too well etched in my facial appearance. The presence of you, Rosamond, would be the finest tonic I know. I freshen quickly--given the proper atmosphere.

Friday night. How I wish you were here! You know, when with you, I am quite impervious to time. I might even be oblivious of surroundings, for you are indeed delightful company.

As I write, a somewhat distracting noise becomes more pronounced in this writing room. The card games carry indications of excitement.

I am not a card player. To some, worldly pursuits are not unlike magnets of irresistible attraction. Those avenues, those circles, exerting a magnetic pull upon ordinary men have little or no influence on me. I find myself in that select group finding their attraction in people of fascinating character.

You, Rosamond, have real attractiveness--an object of beauty, a charm of manner, a personality like a many sided prism--in my youthful eyes.

Your attitude one evening toward me I acknowledge a natural reaction. You called me snobbish. I prefer to term this attitude the legitimate exercise of my refined sense of discrimination. I hope, however, that sophistication isn't so much a part of me, nor my worldliness so keen, as to draw forth a guarded attitude from you forever.

Reflective thought reveals my boastfulness. Now in a ruminating mood, I hope you will not find my boasts too redundant in light of my qualities.

Awake early this morning, I listened to a broadcast of Hitler's speech. So well informed did I consider myself, I dispensed with the customary purchase of "The New York Times."

Early in life I acquired a taste for good living. I deeply appreciate any action or quality meriting that word, "excellence." In thinking of excellence of beauty--I am mindful of a certain Blonde.

Your letters are eagerly awaited. Possessing the natural reflections of a personality of singular charm and sweetness, they provide a source of real pleasure to me, Rosamond.

Reginald

March 24, 1940   New York City, New York

Dear Rosamond

Hello! Here is a big warm greeting, a sincere and cordially appreciative expression of the pleasure that comes to me each and every time a letter from a lovely but shy--and possibly bashful--Rosamond quickens my pulse and gladdens my days.

From the eleventh hour news of the evening, word comes informing us that the temperature in New York is 23 degrees. Temperature of this kind makes the breath congeal in frosty clouds.   You mention summer "seeming" so far away. Such, too are my thoughts. I hope your coming will bring a certain warmth.

The sunshine hasn't been intense but my appearance belies such a statement of facts. My face is just as red as the day I returned from Bermuda--incidentally, that day I set apart in my memory for the pleasure that comes to me in its recall. That day marked the end of the grandest, most pleasurable trip in my life. Such days filled so full to the brim with joy, such days with excitement knowing no bounds, pleasures almost undefinable--all these contributed toward my realization that life can be lordly, sublime--enchanting. Call it tearing a page from a dreamer's existence, term it what you will, I yet will say, moments such as these make one grasp for more.

One of my traits is imagination. Every worthwhile advance in civilization springs from the imagination. A second personal trait is initiative.

Adhering to this second concept, I go to teas, indulge in the artful genialities of the tea room--and if you will believe me, I am rather

201

successful in meeting people. Dr. Fosdick, Dr. Sargent and other of New York's Park Avenue ministers have known me and in the large character of their hospitality have placed their hands on my shoulder and called me, "Son."

I attended a Republican dance at the Waldorf recently. I met most of the swells. Dewey, his attractive wife, many congressmen and other notables attended. Grand music. Swanky crowd. Society in blossom.

I try to force opportunities my way. So did Churchill, so did Chamberlain. There is not a speaker in the Republican party who can match oratorical wits with these two Englishmen. Their great ships are here for safe haven now: Queen Mary, Queen Elizabeth, Mauretania, etc.

Rosamond, you are a well figured attractive girl. A young woman who can write such nice letters as you do has my admiration.

Lovingly,

Reg.

April 22, 1940   New York City, New York

My Dear Rosamond

How thoughtful; how grand of you to have your letter awaiting me this evening on my return from work! These expressions of your thoughts, Sweetheart, strike chords of almost unspeakable joy, awaken a sense of the pleasure a young man experiences in seeing a friendship with some lovely girl nurtured and blossoming forth each month to a degree of perfection comparable only--I add--to the very loveliness of the girl herself.

How delightful of you to write you should like "the most of anything" to see me. Better words, more suitable words, Rosamond Dear, I can no where find to so adequately convey my longing for you. To see you, to awaken mornings and realize you are not 1000 miles distant prompts the wish that July and your coming were the event already of the morrow.

202

The establishment of mutual attachment--one toward the other--is, I hope, no longer conjecture, or speculation with you or me. Altogether, your letter was heart warming. And particularly did I enjoy all the comments descriptive of that grand and <u>lovely blonde</u>, Rosamond. What a pleasure is the knowing of someone who writes with such <u>understanding</u>!

So many of your interests are reflections of mine, so many of your thoughts are ideas long accepted by me that I truly feel I have for a considerable time known you. This has grown into a larger and greater fondness, finding expression only in the word, "Love."

This evening I heard selections from "Sweethearts." Whom was I thinking of? That girl in the picture on my dresser would, if she now turned around, see a sleepy eyed boy. But looking the other way saves her embarrassment for the room is very hot and being ready for bed, I haven't a stitch of clothing on. I believe in comfort. Nothing like ideal conditions.

Without clothing I weigh 180 pounds. How much do you weigh? Do you think I am big enough to hold you? I think I shall try and see what happens. We shall wait and see if you like my physically.

So, to you this night, Darling, I unbosom myself, and wish your soft lips were firmly pressed on mine, signalizing a love mutually reciprocated.

Love,

Reginald

May 12, 1940   New York City, New York

Dear Rosamond

Hello Sweetheart, how are you anyhow! So long have I owed a letter to you I feel honestly as one who has sinned.

Your cheerful letter has brightened my evening just as did its forerunner. You are so kind, so nice to me I can assure you I shall make up for these delays of mine.

How could I best express such gratitude to you? Let me this summer try in my way. And if I do not measure up in the way you would like to have me, you are at liberty in telling me of better ways. You must realize that frankness already binds us together and we must ever tear down and move aside misunderstanding, doubt, hesitancy--in short, we must be free with each other. Now I am warming up; the ink is starting to flow; soon you will know I am in action.

This correspondence surely has not been sustained by any desire for practice in writing, nor has it been maintained by any loneliness on the part of either. It is simply the expression of the longing possessed by each for the possession of the other.

So beautifully do you write, so neatly do you pen your letters, so meticulous is everything attaching to your habits--all these characteristics of yours well up in me an almost indescribably potent admiration.

Just to the extent you give yourself to me will you find in me a strength you have undreamed in the word "reciprocity." Since I have used the word "dreamed," I must be careful for, were I to tell you of some of the dreams in which you were such a lovely figure--dreams in which you figured so large and so beautiful, you would surely say, "Reginald, how could you!"

These exchanges of words would not have originated if you were not a woman and I a man. It is because you have all those things which I haven't that I revel in being a man, for only to man can there be such a lofty appreciation of God's greatest work--woman.

Can you hold your breath for a few moments in a breathless hug when two hearts beat in rhythm, when two bodies know the softness of the other, when two souls speak the same language, when love--and love alone--in the fullness of the moment blackouts life's less exciting adventures?

When anyone stands apart, when one has truly admirable qualities, when one possesses ways so compelling, features and lines of form so perfect, so attracting, I find myself desirous of knowing more intimately that person. I want to make myself a part of that individual. Rosamond, you are that person.

So, until you come, adjectives only can convey what this summer I will impart in person--a love I hope you have not dreamed possible until you have read this.

I am so enjoying our literary intercourse.

Reginald

PS Wait until you have seen the twinkle in my eyes.

May 23, 1940   New York City, New York

Dear Rosamond

Thanks very cordially for your pleasant letter. Your reaction to my last letter was reserved. You are, indeed, reserved to the extreme. Imitation, someone once stated, is the sincerest form of flattery. I shall try to exceed you in this channel. So, if you think our correspondence is having a greater acceleration than our previous face-to-face relationship admits, I shall mollify my efforts and wholly confine my writings to the plane of philosophical and intellectual subjects.

All moods, all feelings, all reactions are possible within each of us when the proper keys are struck. I think we all have the same scale board, but sometimes it is difficult to find in the other person's make-up those keys which we know, when pressed, sound out the desired tune. Haphazardly have I struck a few chords in your heart, but how difficult will it ever be to credit myself with a melody there.

Napoleon is credited with the idea that true friendship requires exchanges of frank expressions of ideas. You see me as somewhat "fast." As a wide-awake youth I soon discovered that I must become formidable competition to other attractive, engaging, and interesting men. In my own way I have learned every trick in the book and have improved upon most of them. I must say--with some boastfulness--that I have become at once a man of the world and the possessor of an enviable cultural background.

Accorded a largeness of hospitality--whether at church teas, cultural circles or in rougher surroundings of a theatrical nature--I must admit that in me there exists no embodiment of the knight of story book chivalry. None whatever. Young women interest me. Some who have many men always at their feet have interest in me.

Now I am in a position to date Park Avenue debutantes, actresses, models, and even the private secretary of David Sarnoff, the president of RCA. With them my conduct is--well, I cannot say and also maintain that new reserve to which I have pledged myself.

But, you wished I confine my remarks to literary expression. Here goes. Girls are being brought into our division at the office for a type of work formerly entrusted only to men of an older age. If war comes, the company does not wish to find itself high and dry. During the last war the company was left in the lurch. They hired a great number of older men. One old fossil was so decrepit he was run over and killed when returning from work one evening.

Churchill is much in the headlines these days. Of all the men living he is the greatest. If England falls, she will have lost with her greatest man at her helm. Unfortunate indeed has been England's tragedy in not heeding the advice of this man of towering and unexcelled prescience. Can you correctly pronounce, "prescience," Rosamond?

Sincerely,

Reginald

"Night of bliss, night of song,
rapturous melody, dreams of pleasure,
oh song of songs,"

come now from the throat of Frank Munn on the radio. Ten o'clock. Too early to "turn in" so I shall go to the Glass Hat, the night club in the hotel one block north. A good orchestra and a big dance floor. If a man can't there enjoy being young, his better years truly have been lived.

206

May 31, 1940   New York City, New York

Dear Rosamond

I have during the past five minutes experienced a pleasure not easily expressed in writing--a pleasure so uplifting--a pleasure so grand, so stimulating that an irresistible "something inside" prompts me to write you, to tell you how glad, how joyed I am over your refreshing letter.

I wish you loved me as I want you to, and in the degree I do you! Knowing you has widened my horizon, my attitude to the appreciation of life. Knowing you has given me a glimpse of how wonderful life can be, how truly glorious and exhiliarating an existence possible when woman and man find themselves gravitating toward each other by forces indescribable, by feelings prompted only by a passioned love.

You think my expressions too amorous. But, Rosamond, you need not fear what you call your "restraint." You will continue to be restrained if -- "inside you"--you find that I am not particularly wonderful. We are both 31. The older one becomes, the more marked the tendency toward weighing one's moves.

I know little of your views. Our limited acquaintance last summer did not permit us to explore the other's thoughts. Time was given only for cursory glances and the exchange of social amenities. Occasionally my letters have turned to ideas of a too adult nature for you. If I appear too personal, please understand that I am only curious about what fascinates me in life.

I would like to know your views on marriage. Are you the kind of a girl who will not marry until you have a Clark Gable, Noel Coward and a John D. Rockefeller all rolled into one? How old do you think you will be before you find a man who is the possessor of such attributes? Before another year rolls around, I am going to be married. Marriage should be bound by a community of interest--music, dancing, literature, and other phases of life. Enjoyment of each other's company and a desire to be part of the other are big factors.

Do you think sex life in marriage one of the most important factors in a successful marriage or do you view it as something to be merely tolerated; something to be put up with as a lesser accompaniment of the night?

I believe there are two kinds of women in this respect. That is: they are either <u>human</u> or else they are <u>priggish old maids</u>. The girl I marry must be human. You can answer these questions without bashfulness. Rosamond, you <u>will</u> answer all these questions if you love me.

You said before that you would rather wait to discuss these things until we can talk personally. If you wish to wait until we can talk, I shall believe that you really do not love me. So, if you prefer to not answer my questions, I shall consider myself relegated to the role of an acquaintance.

Now, Rosamond, I want you to send me a letter that will make me real happy. Please make it soon.

Love,

Reginald Francis Rogers

Rosamond has repeatedly told Reginald that she believes his letter-writing relationship is getting ahead of their actual status as a couple. One can only surmise her response to the previous letter. Whatever the precise content of that letter was, it was sufficiently pointed to prompt Reginald to send the following letter. In order to give the message maximum impact, the letter is delivered to Rosamond as a Western Union telegram--then the fastest way to send a message. Rosamond and Reginald never heard from one another again.

JUNE 6, 1940   NEW YORK CITY, NEW YORK

MISS ROSAMOND BLACKBOURNE=

BECAUSE OF YOUR CONCEPTION OF MY CHARACTER PLEASE FORGET ME=

REGINALD

Arnold Condon playing tourist. He was a solid professional, distinguishing himself as a college professor, author, and musician.

Joyce had gone to the junior prom with Arnold Condon in 1927. They have been seeing each other sporadically for the fourteen years since then. Arnold has not seriously seen another woman during that time. Joyce has been pursued by a fellow teacher in Goodman, Wisconsin, for whom she has reciprocal feelings. She has not allowed this relationship with Mr. Werner to come to fruition because he is a beer drinker and not a Methodist, and she knows her parents would not approve. And so Joyce and Arnold continue along as something of a couple, as if by default.

In this letter Joyce tells of her return to her teaching job after spending Christmas vacation in Brodhead. Arnold was in Brodhead on vacation from his teaching position as well. The couple has made a somewhat circuitous trip back to their respective communities, going by way of Milwaukee for an evening of dancing at a hotel ballroom.

January 4, 1941   Hortonville, Wisconsin

Dear Mama and Papa,

I returned to H (don't you think that's a good name for this place?) at 6:15 this morning. I was just in time to change my clothes, wash my face and go to church. We had an uneventful train ride from Brodhead to Milwaukee. We danced until the orchestra quit. Then Arnold took me in a taxi over to the station so I could take my train up north and he was going to walk over to the North Shore depot to take their last train for Chicago. It was quite the long night.

Now this p.m. I am sleepy. I think I will take a nap and get rested up for school tomorrow.

Thank you for a lovely Christmas celebration and the nice gifts.

Love,

Joyce

This letter is written on what is arguably the most significant date in the twentieth century--with momentous events occurring at a place called Pearl Harbor. Arnold, of course, has not yet heard the news broadcasts at the time of writing.

The letter typifies the cordial but unimpassioned seventeen-year courtship which Arnold and Joyce endured between their first teenage date and their middle-age marriage. The level of intensity of their relationship did not create the flurries of letters which Rosamond received.

December 7, 1941   Iowa City, Iowa

Dear Joyce,

Well how are you? And, how do you like teaching by now? I like Iowa **(the University at Iowa City)** *the best of any place I have taught.*

When we are both home over Christmas, would you like to spend a day together? We could take the train to Chicago and take in a matinee at one of the theaters, then have dinner at a fancy place, and still get back to Brodhead before it is too terribly late.

I hope all is well with your folks,

Arnold

Now four years have passed since the "Reginald Interlude" in Rosamond's life. In vivid contrast to Reginald's New York sophistication, his colorful prose, and his ego now comes a new suitor characterized by down-home simplicity. He's Kenneth Jordan--one of Rosamond's high school classmates, and a Brodhead insurance agent. They are both 35; both single.

Ken is a truly nice man. He's genuinely friendly, honest, and caring. The courtship lasts only a few months before Rosamond concludes it. Perhaps Ken's writing about blisters on his heels is just a little too much of a contrast with the refinements to which Rosamond has grown accustomed. As with the Reginald letters, the few Kenneth letters are presented together here without further commentary.

January 7, 1944   Brodhead, Wisconsin

Dear Rosamond:

It sure was good to happen to see you downtown when you were home to Brodhead for the holidays. I would like to see you again and have a chance to talk with you. Let me know the next time you will be coming to Brodhead. Maybe I could meet you at the bus.

Sincerely,

Kenneth

February 15, 1944   Brodhead, Wisconsin

Dear Rosamond

I want to thank you for the nice valentine you sent me. I sure appreciated it. You sure were a good girl to save your candy until Feb. 14. Don't worry about me not sharing it with you as I weigh too much already.

When you come home next time I want you to come over to my house for dinner. I sure enjoyed the little time we had together a week ago.

I hope you will not wait too long before you come home again. I enjoy being with you.

Sincerely,

Kenneth

March 25, 1944   Brodhead, Wisconsin

Dear Rosamond:

I have been thinking of the wonderful time we had together last Sunday. I hope we will have many more of them. I am looking forward to warmer weather when we can spend the Sunday in some park. If you have a picture of yourself that I can have I would appreciate it. Do not fail to let me know when you are coming home again.

As ever,

Kenneth

June 4, 1944   Brodhead, Wisconsin

Dear Rosamond:

Just thought I would write you a line before leaving Philadelphia. We have been over to Independence Hall and have walked past the Insurance Company of North America building. I sure have enjoyed Philadelphia. Yesterday we went through the Betsy Ross house. I am leaving this PM at 6:22 on the Trail Blazer for Chicago. It is sure a nice train to ride on. I have walked so much that I have two water blisters on each heel. I will write you another letter when I get back to Brodhead. Carl is putting his military return address on the letter so that I will not need a stamp. I don't suppose I should beat the government out of the revenue.

Sincerely,

Kenneth

July 14, 1944   Brodhead, Wisconsin

Dear Rosamond:

It sure was good to see you again but I was sorry to hear you can't keep on dating me. I understand there's the distance and the difference in the places we want to live. You are a very sweet girl, Rosamond, and I have thought about you all the time. I liked our times together. There wasn't anything I liked better than that. I sure looked forward to those Fridays when I would meet you at the bus.

With the best of love,

Kenneth

The next letter from Arnold to Joyce is written during their engagement. Arnold is already living in Arizona, and he writes to Joyce in Brodhead. She is a teacher at Brodhead High School and living with her parents. For a letter passing between lovers who are engaged to be married, it is markedly devoid of emotion or personal commentary. Such would be the nature of their relationship.

September 24, 1944   Tucson, Arizona

Dearest Joyce

I am up in my office supposedly working but I guess I had better drop you a few lines to let you know that I am still on earth.

Well, let me see what have I done since I last wrote. I kept on looking at houses--most of them no good. I worked up here yesterday until noon. Then I sun bathed, swam and showered. Then I went to the faculty dinner.

The party was quite nice. We had cocktails and I got kidded plenty for not taking one. Hamburgers with onions, hot sauce, salad, corn, toasted buns, olives, and chocolate cake with whipped cream. It was really quite nice.

Not very exciting, huh? It seems as though I don't accomplish as much as I should. Hope I get on the beam **(an aviation term meaning "on course")** *a little, of course, I never was one to work entirely!*

Love, Arnold

These romantic letters have encompassed a mere six years--the years of World War II, coincidentally. When this brief era began, the United States was one of half a dozen nations comprising the top echelon of military powers.

Economically, the United States possessed the capacity to be the world's leader of production; but the American consciousness was far more focused on the privations of the recent Great Depression than it was upon material potential.

Socially, the era began with the sanctity of the American family institutionally intact. Some married after thoughtful consideration; some married in flippant haste. Some married to fulfill a deep and abiding love; others married to serve shallow agendas. But, virtually all married for permanence. Marriage was a sacred trust--the same as parenting, the same as earning a livelihood, the same as defending the Republic.

By the end of this brief historical interlude, the United States was one of *two* contenders for top military recognition. Economically, the nation ended the era twice as rich as it had begun. The world envied American productivity and would soon be clamoring for American cars, blue jeans, and TV sets.

Socially, American dreams leaped boundlessly in terms of what was expected from life--material well-being, good times, satisfying relationships.

Right on cue with the national trend, Rosamond tried and rejected several relationships before choosing a husband; and Joyce soon pulled out of a marriage that failed to deliver what she thought had been promised. Their experiences were just the tip of a sociological iceberg which would displace much of the traditional thinking about relationships.

215

CHAPTER NINE

THE POST-WAR ERA, 1946-1984

The life of the Blackbourne family changes drastically following World War II. The cast of people living in the old Brodhead home changes as one generation is supplanted by the next.

This chapter concludes the Blackbourne generations. Joyce will marry in 1945 and Rosamond in 1948. The only member of the fourth generation of the Brodhead home, Gregg, will be born in 1947.

Addie will die relatively young in 1949; and Loudon will live a long and healthy life, still operating his business on his last living day at age 84.

The fifth generation--Gregg's sons, Scott and Todd--will be born in 1976 and 1978, and their letters to their grandparents will be the concluding letters in this book.

And as always, the rolling drama of the American people is played out over the decades. Here is a young man's dissatisfaction with college life in the 1960s--a vivid contrast to the concerns of young members of the family in the 1860s when Wesley Smith faced rebel gunfire or the 1850s when Daniel Burdick planned to buy a new team of horses so he could do man's work.

This is the first letter which Joyce sends to Rosamond after she and Arnold move into their new house in Tucson. Interestingly, she mentions the price of the lot, the house, and the furniture. Arnold was sending the bills for the house to his mother, as she had pledged to pay for their new house. Only trouble was, that made it *mother's* house in mother's viewpoint; and *that* eventually became the "last straw" in Joyce's marriage.

The "egg woman" is a person who sells eggs and regularly delivers them to her customers.

January 26, 1946   Tucson, Arizona

Dearest Roman (Joyce and Rosamond were both Latin teachers)

I find the time now to send you "a line." How are you? I suppose you are home. Then no doubt you know that. Ha. Ha.

This a.m. we--no, make that I--cleaned up the house. It looks so nice when it is clean & so messy otherwise. I got lunch for Arnold. He is dieting so we eat fruit & vegetables for lunch. We had potato chips, cole slaw, celery, carrot sticks, half a grapefruit & a cookie.

He sunbathed on a blanket on the terrace from 12:05 --1:10 & I stayed in the sun a little while then mended stockings. Then the egg woman came and brought her sister. I asked them if they wanted to see the house. I knew they did. They will bring chicken manure with the eggs any time we want it. Mighty big of them I'd say.

Arnold got back at 3:00 so he could type the figures of the bills & a letter to his mother. The lot cost $750, the furniture $1400, and the house $11,000.

I went to the Market Spot where you go in and pick up what you want instead of having a clerk wait on you. I got 3 lbs. of brown sugar and 7 of white. The newspaper says that in February & March there will be a sugar shortage.

"Guest Wife" with Claudette Colbert was the most humorous and entertaining of any show I have seen for a long time. You would like it.

Love,

Joyce

This letter from Joyce to her parents tells something of Joyce's life in Arizona. Her husband, in addition to being the chairman of the Business Education Department at the University of Arizona, also has a job playing saxophone in a nightclub band five nights a week.

And, since the home is technically the property of Arnold's mother, she has insisted that the young couple initiate some economy measures. One such strategem has been to rent out a bedroom. So, Arnold and Joyce have dutifully rented a room to two elderly Jewish sisters recently arrived from war-ravaged Europe.

January 30, 1946   Tucson, Arizona

Dearest Mama & Papa,

How are you?

This a.m. the sidewalk was put in. The clothesline was put up Sunday afternoon. No sooner are we here than our renters have moved in. The ladies are nice. The older one wants to tell stories all the time & I feel I have something else to do all the time. You know how 'tis. I should think she would get on her sister's nerves, but I suppose she is used to it. We got a bunch of 19 bananas downtown & gave them three.

Arnold has been playing saxophone with the university band, most recently for a veterans' dance. The enrollment has gone up a lot with veterans returning from the war. Last night Arnold played at the "Blue Moon" for pay. The leader wants five saxes and wants Arnold to be part of the band permanently. I went with him to the "Moon" & sat & watched. It was over at 11:30 and the bus got us here about 12.

Arnold teaches all day, practices with the Univ. band at 4:40, then goes to play with the professional band in the evenings. I am to have supper ready to pop into his mouth when he arrives at 5:45.

Much love,

Joyce

John Plichta at the time he met Rosamond. He always had a merry twinkle in his eye and a smile for everybody.

In 1947, Rosamond finally meets the man she is destined to marry. She has just moved to Milwaukee suburb, West Allis, to teach in the high school. There she meets John Plichta. He is the history teacher and football coach. He has been a college football player, semi-pro baseball player, and Olympic ski jumper. He is a health fanatic and is as fit and trim as a 47-year old can be. Nine years older than Rosamond, he has been single for 12 years since his first wife died in childbirth.

John is a real "people person." He delights in bringing a smile to the face of people he meets. He delights in life itself, and is fascinated by much. He is great with children, often joining in their play. He exhibits a great sense of humor.

Because John and Rosamond live in the same community, their courtship isn't generating many letters. Two letters, however, did find their way into safe keeping in the attic.

John and Rosamond met in the autumn of 1946, and on the following February 9 he proposed marriage. It was the day of the remarriage of Joe and Nellie Blackbourne after their 50-year divorce.

The first of the pair of letters is written following John's first weekend visit to Rosamond's parents' home in Brodhead. Rosamond's cousin, Lyle Blackbourne, the football coach at Marquette University in 1947 is destined to become the coach of the Green Bay Packers in the early fifties.

January 6, 1947   West Allis, Wisconsin

Dear Rosamond, though I think I would rather call you "Rose Blossom."

What a nice time I had with you and your folks. Your mama cooks a real good meal. I don't know when I ate so much roast beef as I did at her Sunday dinner. That's another thing we have in common. My mama is a real good cook too. Having English parents, you've never had good Czech home cooking, I'll bet. I'll have to ask my mother to cook a meal for us.

Give my thanks to your parents. They have a real comfortable home to be in and I was made to feel real welcome. Your father seemed to get a real kick out of the fact that I had played college football opposite his nephew.

I'll be looking forward to having you return to West Allis. I think the sky is bluer and the snow is whiter when you are in town.

Love

John

This letter is written a few weeks prior to the marriage of John and Rosamond. He writes the letter purely in the spirit of fun, and it reveals his twinkle-in-the-eye personality. Having lost his first wife in childbirth, John is afraid to try parenthood again. And so this couple which has the ideal temperament for parenthood remains childless. Gregg will revel in their company and consider them to be his second set of parents. Indeed, he is destined to have more healthy good times with this set of pseudo parents than he will have with his own.

This letter characterizes yet another distinctly unique personality. The love letters to Rosamond and Joyce portray the great differences among people. Reginald wrote letters which were passionate and eager, Ken wrote with uncomplicated sincerity and simplicity, Arnold's writing has shown him to be cordial yet distant, and John's writing is an expression of acceptance and fun.

May 27, 1948   West Allis, Wisconsin

Dear Rosamond,

Pardon me for writing on the back of a student's test paper. There must be a paper shortage in this country. I do hope we don't go back to writing on stone. That would be tough on envelopes.

I believe that the number one problem in our marriage will be to keep the rug on the stairs looking new. The best way to keep that stair rug looking new, is not to step on it. As I see it, there are two ways to get to the second floor without abusing the stair rug!

Method Number One. Ask for permission to use the neighbor's stairs. The only problem is that you would then be on the second floor of the wrong house. Suggestion number one is, therefore, null and void and should be exterminated, discarded, and completely cast out from further consideration. Scrap it.

Method Number Two. Crawl up the banister to get from the first floor to the second; slide down the banister to get from the second floor to the first. But be careful, Rosamond, in climbing up because sometimes you might find me sliding down and that would create a most abrupt and compromising situation. It's one of my guiding principles in life to never slide down a banister that is occupied by a woman whose sole ambition is to reach the top.

Should we have a collision on the banister (there is only one "n" in banister), we must be certain to drop to the floor below and not on the stair rug.

In the case of a family dispute, Rosamond, never run for the stairs. Fight it out in the kitchen like a real woman, and if you need weaponry you can grab a frying pan and chase me down the alley.

That is the way to save wear on the new stair rug!

Lovingly, John

This letter from Rosamond to Joyce reveals that Joyce's family is not making it easy for her to live in Arizona. Inspired by an overly keen sense of sentiment, they keep tugging at her heart strings. Arnold's mother has gone to stay with Joyce and Arnold, and the couple is traveling one of marriage's rockier roads. Rosamond will not mention Arnold in her letters to Joyce for a dozen years.

September 4, 1948   Brodhead, Wisconsin

Dearest Joyce and Grrr-egg,

John and I are in Brodhead visiting the folks. We keep thinking about you and talking about you & feeling sorry for you in your progress to hotter realms.

John wishes that little Gregg were here. He misses him and he would just like to "squeeze him up." We got here yesterday. John had bought tomatoes and sweet corn to bring. Last evening for supper we had tomatoes, sweet corn, and peach sundaes for dessert.

Hope you and Gregg will stay healthy.   I love you both a lot--the dearest and the best. Give Gregg a good hug and kiss from his aunt.

Rosamond

Joyce Condon with Gregg in Tucson, Arizona in 1948.

223

Rosamond writes to Joyce a short time after her wedding. The letter includes insights into the polio scare and incomes. Rosamond mentions her new home as being in a quiet country location. Today it is deep within the metropolitan area, with true rural conditions being a great many miles distant.

September 16, 1948   West Allis, Wisconsin

Dearest Joyce & Grrr-egg,

Three weeks ago today at this time we were just winding up with the wedding pictures. It really seems like a long time already.

I am at present sitting under the hair dryer and trying to economize on time. A year ago on the first full moon in the fall John took me on my first moonlight convertible ride. We both remembered it and concluded that being married to each other is better than not.

John is very nice and lots of fun. I am still glad I married him. That is a good thing, isn't it? I tell him he's my favorite husband and he laughs. John wishes that Gregg lived closer so that he could play with him. He missed him a lot the last time we were out to Brodhead.

It is so wonderful going out to work on our new place. It takes me only 20 minutes by bus. In that short a space of time, all the rumble of the city ceases and I can walk in a quiet country spot. I'll be glad when you can visit us.

Tomorrow we get our first paycheck & we will be glad. I'll earn $376.20 per month, which is $3,385.80 for the year. So you were meditating on a $2100 job. You want <u>bigger</u> money than that passing through your fingers. Ha!

The grade schools in Milwaukee County aren't opening yet this Monday. Polio is still bad. They cancelled all High School football games & dances & the kids aren't allowed in the pool.

Keep on writing. Love you & Gregg

Rosamond

Addie's letter to Joyce gives a perspective on many of the details in everyday life at mid-twentieth century.

September 20, 1948   Brodhead, Wisconsin

Dear little Joyce:-

Saturday after I picked up your letter at the P.O.   I went over to Helen's. I took her a little jar of jam I had made. I haven't done anything with peaches or tomatoes yet. I spent Saturday evening at the store. Papa sold some wall paper. I didn't get home till nearly eleven. Papa came before a great while.

Yesterday morning papa decided Puppy should have a bath so I helped him in the back yard. We got along fine.

Today we went to the Coffee Shop for dinner. They had chicken. You really get better there for $1.25 than you do at the "Dog House," and you don't have to eat pie or pay extra for ice cream. It was better than at the Monroe hotel for $1.50.

Sunday we went visiting the folks over around Woodford. It was hard work for papa driving over those terrible hills and awful ruts. Then the car got to smelling so and the oil seemed to be given out. So he stopped at a place and nobody home but the dogs. We stopped at another place with the same result. Then we stopped at a prosperous looking place and papa was able to buy two quarts of oil.

Henry and Hazel asked us to stay all night but we left Puppy in the house and papa had to open the store Monday morning.

I must quit and write a line to Rosamond.

Mother

This letter from Rosamond to sister, Joyce, recalls that world apart from our own when big-city shopping entailed trolley cars,

225

department stores, and downtown. The first paragraph is written to Gregg, even though he's a year old and obviously won't be reading it.

September 27, 1948   West Allis, Wisconsin

Dearest Joyce and Grrr-egg,

I am glad you have grown so nice & straight, Grrr, and can eat almost everything you like. I should think that would make it much easier for you now if you don't have to bother with special baby food any more.

John and I have been doing lots of stuff at the new house. We stood at the bottom of the stairs looking at the new carpet and we had a good laugh. The reason is one of those "long stories" you hear about.

Thursday night I went downtown and over to Schuester's department store. Of course if I were using proper Milwaukee language I would say "I went down by Schuesters." I always get a kick out of hearing Milwaukeeans talk. While I was waiting for the streetcar a man in the crowd approached another and said, "Why don't you hello me when you know me so easy?"

I bought us a bed spread--white chenille with rose trim--the prettiest I could find. I got a plastic bath room curtain, white with roses on it. I try to get the prettiest and cutest of everything--more fun that way.

Lots of love to you both,

Rosamond

This is Addie's last letter. She is a very aged 73. She has suffered a stroke, though nobody knows it yet. She doesn't know what is wrong with her, and hasn't consulted a doctor. (There is no health insurance, and ordinary folks are in no hurry to spend money on doctor visits for ailments which may pass of their own accord.) She dies the next day in her beloved home--in the same room where she has slept since she was a little girl, the same room where she was a new bride, the same room where she had delivered her babies.

August 7, 1949   Brodhead, Wisconsin

Dear Rosamond,

Well you can see by my handwriting something is terribly wrong. I am shaking all over and can't seem to stop it. Yesterday I got a terrible pain in my head and it only seems to get worse. I can scarcely get up from a chair and can't do anything. Papa has to be at the store so he asked Harvey Day to come sit with me a while.

I don't know what we'll do if I can't do the house work. We're in an awful fix.

I hope you can come see me soon.

Lovingly,

Your mother

When Joyce returns to Brodhead for her mother's funeral, she and Gregg remain in the old home with Loudon. Arnold and Joyce will not divorce, but their relationship will be on a level which might be expected between distant cousins. It will be only after Arnold's mother dies 30 years later that they get back together and resume what appears to be a normal marriage.

Arnold has just moved from the University of Arizona to the University of Illinois. The following letter sets the tone of their marriage for the next third of a century.

September 15, 1950   Urbana, Illinois

Dear Joyce,

Well, by now it is pretty clear that you have every intention of staying in Brodhead. I can't tell my mother to leave; she needs someone to take care

of her. So she can live with me and you can live with your father. I think
you are happier that way anyway.

I think Gregg will get a poor start in life growing up in a small town.
There are so many advantages for him in a college town with a professor
for a father. But I won't fight you for custody of him.

We can have some weekends together when mother and I come to stay at
her house in Brodhead. Maybe our relationship will be like a permanent
honeymoon if we aren't together all the time.

Let's stick it out for another year anyway and see what happens. I do love
you.

Arnold

**During the 30 years that Arnold and Joyce did not live together, they
rarely spent time together. When they did, the occasion could end
with hard feelings. Yet, most of the time their relationship was
cordial and polite. Here Arnold, now 46, has taken a
business/vacation trip to New York City and writes a post card to
Joyce and Gregg.**

December 5, 1955

Dear Joyce & Gregg:

*Well, I really had a day of it--Slept as late as I wanted to--12 noon. Read
N.Y. Times a little & then walked downtown. Saw Katherine Dunham's
dance review. Then to Radio City show & then to "Guys & Dolls"--Now
getting an oyster stew before going to bed. Have lunch with publisher
tomorrow, then to Atlantic City tomorrow night. Hope you are all ok.*

Love

Arnold

This letter from Rosamond when Gregg is 13 bespeaks her values, her personality, and their relationship.

March 22, 1961   West Allis, Wisconsin

Dearest Gregg,

Congratulations on your first place rating on your clarinet solo. I wish that I could have heard you. I'm glad to hear you did so well and made all your relatives so proud of you.

Thanks so much for your letter and your invitation to come see you join the church. I should like to be there for that because I know it will keep you a better man always. But I guess probably we had better not try it this weekend, because there is work we should do here and we'll be coming out there Thursday night anyway.

John and I both enjoyed your letter a lot and did not have to wake each other up while reading it. You are quite a writer. I feel as though I should write you a letter like you did, only I am not clever enough to think of so many peculiar and funny ways to state things.

I must go to school now to heckle some poor kids. Much love to you, your mama, and my papa.

The "ant"

This letter from Gregg shows a young person's uncertainty about choosing a course in life. Further, it shows a disillusionment with the process of higher education--a keen sense of disappointment that stayed with him throughout his academic career.

Despite initial misgivings, Gregg stayed with his studies and eventually earned a doctor's degree and became a professor. He felt that his initial instincts about the nature of education were vindicated when his university students would often say, "Your course is what I expected college to be like."

October 14, 1965

Dear Mom,

Well, here I am at college. I can't say I like it much. College kids are just that, kids. They act like eighth-graders one minute, and then act like the great intellectual critics of society the next.

Me? I'm ready for a nice house in the suburbs. You know, a nice workshop for my hobbies, plenty of room for my books, a good chair by a fireplace. The idea of living like a rat in a little hole of a dorm room for the next four years doesn't appeal to me in the least.

I don't know if college is for me. I always thought a university was a place for the exchange of ideas and that the great variety of ideas to which one is exposed expands his intellect. I <u>thought</u> that grades would be based on how well you frame an argument--you know, how well you can express yourself and how well you can substantiate your view.

The other day I wrote an essay in which I knew I was disagreeing with the professor, but I supported my view with quotes from Shakespeare, Lincoln, and the Bible. I thought I did a great job of being a fledgling intellectual, but I received no credit for my answer. The moron professor wrote, "What's this? It isn't in the book." Is that all this business is about? Dumbly repeating what's in a book? Socrates wouldn't have thought so. Too bad Socrates isn't a professor at UW Madison. Ha Ha

Love,

Gregg

In the next letter Joyce writes to her son, Gregg, just prior to his college graduation with a bachelor's degree. She refers to "Pop," Gregg's name for his grandfather Blackbourne.

May 14, 1970   Brodhead, Wisconsin

Dearest Gregg,

So you've made it to college graduation; well, close enough that we'll say you're there. I want you to know I'm so proud of you. It hasn't been easy, but you've done it. I know your father is also proud. Pop would have been, too.

I believe you are doing what God instructs us to do in the parable of the "talents." That is, that we are to give back to God a good return on what he has invested in us. I am glad you are going to be a teacher like so many of your relatives. A teacher has the perfect opportunity to make a difference in the lives of others.

With a mother's love,

Mom

Gregg Condon at age 35 was a professor at the University of Wisconsin-Eau Claire and the third-generation author of the Gregg Shorthand series of textbooks.

For 30 years Arnold and Joyce were apart. Loudon Blackbourne died in 1963. When Alice Condon died in 1979, Arnold and Joyce began living together again. In old age they began to express affection for each other. Indeed, they came to rely on one another. When Arnold died in 1996, Joyce followed him a mere six weeks later.

Scott and Todd had only known the elder Condons to have a "normal" relationship; and to them, trips to grandma and grandpa's house were great fun.

December 25, 1982   Brodhead, Wisconsin

Dear Joyce,

I didn't buy a Christmas card because I wanted to give you one which you would know was straight from the heart. You are my sweetheart. I am glad we are married and I am enjoying the good times we have together. I believe you are too.

Love

Arnold.

Scott and Todd are the fifth generation of the family to celebrate Christmas in the old house in Brodhead. Here six-year-old Scott writes to Arnold and Joyce.

December 30, 1982   Altoona, Wisconsin

Dear Grandma and Grandpa,

Thank you for the nice Christmas presents. I had a nice time at Christmas at your house. I liked the turkey. You can come see us sometime.

Love,

Scott Condon

Arnold and Joyce as grandparents continued the fine traditions of the old family home.

Todd and Scott Condon at Grandma and Grandpa's house in 1984. Their letters were the sixth generation's letters to occupy a place in the attic.

The last letter in this volume is to Arnold and Joyce from grandson, Todd, who is six. It is a fitting conclusion to our investigation of six generations' lives, for it is the world seen through the eyes of one whose life has just begun--it's a perspective that's bright, cheerful, and positive.

August 8, 1984   Altoona, Wisconsin

Dear Grandma and Grandpa

We are home now. It was nice to visit your house. I liked going to the lake to. I liked swiming and riding in the boat. Im glad you like milk shakes grandpa because i do to. I will come see you again sometime. Here is a picture i made of your hapy house.

Love

Todd

More than a century after Francis and Hannah Smith built their house, great-great grandson Todd characterizes his ancestral home as a happy place.

234

Francis and Hannah Smith built their dream home 117 years before their great-great grandson, Todd, wrote the final letter which appears in this volume. His six-year-old observation of their home being a "hapy house" is a tribute to them and a testament to the value of the American family.

EPILOGUE

The letters from the attic of the old home in Brodhead, Wisconsin told the story of six generations of one American family. The earliest letters were written by people born in the 1700s, people whose parents had fought in the American Revolution. The letters continued in unbroken sequence down to the present generation who are still young. The letters told the story of five generations' privilege to call the same house, "home."

It has been said that those who do not know history are doomed to repeat it. That pessimistic view focuses on the negatives in history. This book has been about the positives in history--the positives of perseverance, of industry, of faith, and of love. Looking at history optimistically, then, we might fear that those who do not know history will *fail* to repeat it.

Letters From the Attic has not been the story of the rare famous people who made headlines, but the story of the ordinary hard-working people who made the American dream come true. The letters have provided a window to the glow of a certain greatness of spirit which can be kindled in the hearts of ordinary men and women. It is a spirit which transcends title, wealth, or power. It is a greatness which all people are equally free to live out if they can only first grasp it in their minds. Addie talked about it in her 1893 high school commencement address:

> *The greatest monuments are not monuments of stone. The greatest monuments are monuments of the human heart.*
>
> *Build a monument of heart, mind, and soul in whose light future generations will find their way.*
>
> *After the work of the ages is done, it will be seen that ordinary people have built the greatest monuments of all.*

236

OLD SAYINGS AND FIGURES OF SPEECH

Following is a list of archaic expressions. They are in chronological order. Each listing includes the year, the expression, and (where appropriate) a translation in 1990's verbiage.

1853 *atall*
        at all

1853 *sling snot*
        gossip

1853 *so she may set that down*
        so she may remember that

1853 *western wilds*
        Wisconsin

1853 *John used her very mean*
        John was mean to her

1853 *put the children out*
        find other places for the children to live

1853 *he is a going to break up housekeeping*
        he is not going to have a place of his own to live

1853 *we went to meeting*
        we went to church

1853 *he is worth a considerable property*
        he has a lot of property

1853   *it is most church*
       it is almost time for church to start

1853   *I sewed a piece of oats*
       I planted a field of oats

1853   *the boy is destined to be more dummy than prophet*

1853   *I am writing to you according to contract*
       I am writing to you as I promised

1853   *hollowing like a good fellow*
       hollering like a strong man

1853   *lay yourself out for a sign*
       lie down so we notice you

1853   *I broke his heart so he couldn't eat anything but lemon pie for six weeks*

1853   *a quill popgun*
       (Research found no such firearm.)

1853   *I'd like a specimen of your handwriting*
       Please write to me

1853   *I commenced my school*
       my school started

1853   *I called in*
       I stopped in

1853   *I found my plantation in good order*
       my crops are growing well

1853   *Scolding trim*
       crabby mood

1853   *a running, a working, a keeping, etc.*
          running, working, keeping, etc.

1853   *she jaws at everyone*
          she scolds everyone

1854   *it devolved upon me to purpose for it*
          I'm the one who had to do it

1854   *ma is a churning and the butter is most come*
          mother is making butter and it's almost done

1854   *he can't do the first hands turn of chores*
          he can't do a bit of work

1854   *he killed his pork today*
          he butchered hogs today

1854   *everyone has got western fever*
          everyone wants to move out west

1854   *I hope I may live to see you*

1854   *the house and barn when built will be worth $500*

1854   *we will get some walnuts and have a good cracking*

1854   *blackberry time*
          when the blackberries are ripe

1854   *it's most church again*
          it's nearly time for church again

1854   *I want going*
          I wasn't going

1854   *We've got candidates from all four parties--Hards, No-Nothings,*
          Whigs, and Democrats.

239

1854   *ain't that a buster*
       isn't that funny

1854   *more properly speaking*
       to put it better

1854   *How are you a gettin along?*
       How are you doing?

1854   *the streets were full of beer and gingerbread stands*

1854   *our Sabbath school will have an exhibition*
       our Sunday school will have a program

1854   *her dress cost 6 and 6 pence a yard*
       her dress cost six shillings and six pence a yard (In English
       measure there are 12 pence to a shilling and 20 shillings to a
       pound.)

1854   *she bought her a new dress*
       she bought a new dress for herself

1854   *I went around a good deal with pa*
       I traveled with dad

1854   *he keeps house in Joe's place*
       he lives in Joe's house

1854   *I will send money in a certificate*
       I will send a check

1854   *a very open winter*
       not much snow

1854   *I loathe the idea*
       I hate the idea

1854   *draw writings*
       prepare a contract

1854   *carry me*
       give me a ride

1854   *trees are leaving out*
       trees are leafing out

1854   *your good by land*
       your destination

1854   *I got the 80 for $7.50*
       I bought 80 acres for $7.50

1854   *I sold the team of oxen for $140.*

1854   *I pay for hands 50 cents haying*
       I pay 50 cents a day to hired help for haying

1854   *large scholars*
       children in upper grades

1854   *mitts and cloak*
       mittens and coat

1854   *Calvin is sparking Mary*
       Calvin is dating Mary

1855   *to bring up their candidate*
       to promote their candidate

1855   *bile*
       boil

1855   *I'm about for going into a store.*
       I'm thinking of working in a store.

1855   *I experienced religion*
       I accepted faith in God

1855   *she has got a crow for a man*
      her fiance is not good looking

1855   *yours of the 15th came to hand*
      I received your letter of the 15th

1855   *feeling quite smart*
      feeling well

1855   *made you a visit*
      paid you a visit

1855   *cholera season*
      hot weather

1855   *I 'low*
      a contraction of "I allow," meaning "I guess"

1855   *mother is as good as pie*
      mother is very well

1857   *I have concluded to write*
      I have decided to write

1857   *hitch traces*
      get married

1857   *I'd like to see his tobacco soaker*
      I'd like to see his face

1857   *all I have pressed through*
      all I have endured

1857   *I bid all dull care begone*
      I'm determined to be positive

1858   *she has taken up with your advice*
      she has taken your advice

1858   *according to the dispensations of providence*
       by the grace of God

1858   *I'm fixin to buy me a team*
       I'm planning to buy a team of horses.

1858   *What are hogs on the cars?*
       What price is being paid for hogs loaded on the train?

1858   *I'm for clerking it in a store.*
       I want to work as a store clerk.

1858   *we begin to hear the factory bells*
       factories are operating again following a business depression

1858   *hurry up your cakes*
       get pregnant soon

1858   *I am bound to put er through*
       I am determined to finish

1858   *I hardly know what I am about*
       I hardly know what I am doing

1859   *we are all well as common*
       our health is normal

1859   *humbug*
       rumor

1859   *get spliced*
       get married

1863   *they was a visitor*
       there was a visitor

1863   *we go fetch in a hog*
       we go get a hog

1863 *your letter came at hand last night*
    I got your letter last night

1864 *long ere this*
    long before this

1864 *yours received*
    I got your letter

1892 *I'm digging out a little*
    I'm getting better

1892 *I can hardly stir*
    I can hardly move

1894 *so I can beat the train*
    so I can get to the station before the train does

1894 *things were very gay*
    things were very festive

1894 *Cecie is a bed*
    Cecie is in bed

1899 *common school*
    grade school

1906 *just got your postal*
    I just received your letter

1906 *having little trade*
    having few customers

1906 *remember me to mom*
    tell mom hi for me

1906 *I had a caller today*
    I had a visitor today

| 1908 | *you'll make a storekeeper o k* |
| | you'll succeed in business |

1916 *cuddles and love*

| 1916 | *scratch up* |
| | hurry up |

| 1916 | *put her on a tonic* |
| | prescribed a medicine for her |

| 1923 | *if you have any desire to go on in this world* |
| | if you care to succeed |

| 1927 | *my spook will be with you* |
| | I will be with you in spirit |

| 1927 | *it acted like a storm* |
| | I thought it would rain |

| 1927 | *I'm kind of up a stump* |
| | I'm rather confused |

| 1927 | *the house is as still as the tomb* |
| | the house is as quiet as a tomb |

| 1927 | *the bed laid awful good* |
| | the bed felt comfortable |

| 1928 | *mosey up here* |
| | walk up here |

| 1939 | *I will not gain say* |
| | I will not disagree |

| 1939 | *such untoward incidents* |
| | such improper incidents |

1939 *send me a portrait of yourself*
   send me a picture of yourself

1939 *I freshen quickly*
   I rest up quickly

1944 *go take a sun bath*
   go lie out in the sun

1945 *I shouldn't work myself out so*
   I shouldn't work so hard

1946 *the egg woman*
   the woman who sells eggs

1948 *the oil gave out*
   we ran out of oil

1948 *I wrote to Mr. Sears*
   I ordered from the Sears catalog

1948 *I fairly get the blahs*
   I often get depressed

1948 *we turned on the cooler*
   we turned on the air conditioner

1948 *aired the bedding*
   hung the sheets on the clothesline

1948 *played out*
   over tired